The Architecture of
BOHLIN CYWINSKI JACKSON

with essays by Joseph Esherick and Mack Scogin

First published in the United States of America by:
Rockport Publishers, Inc.
146 Granite Street
Rockport, Massachusetts 01966
Telephone: (508) 546-9590
Fax: (508) 546-7141
Telex: 5106019284 ROCKORT PUB

Distributed to the book trade and art trade
in the U.S. and Canada by:
The American Institute of Architects Press
1735 New York Avenue NW
Washington, DC 20006
Telephone: (800) 365-2724

Other Distribution by:
Rockport Publishers, Inc.
Rockport, Massachusetts 01966

ISBN 1-55835-121-3

10 9 8 7 6 5 4 3 2

Author: Bohlin Cywinski Jackson
Art Direction & Design: Laura Herrmann
Production Manager: Barbara States
Production Assistant: Pat O'Maley
Cover Photographs: Front cover — Software Engineering Institute, Pittsburgh, PA (Joint Venture with Burt Hill Kosar Rittelmann Associates); Back cover (top to bottom) — Harrisburg Airport Terminal, Middletown, PA; Summer House, West Cornwall, CT; Pennsylvania Higher Education Assistance Agency, Harrisburg, PA; Residential Compound Guest House, Medina, WA (Joint Venture with James Cutler Architects); Pool Pavilion, Montgomery County, PA; Shelly Ridge Girl Scout Center, Miquon, PA; Center for Biotechnology and Bioengineering, Pittsburgh, PA.
All photographs by Karl A. Backus except back cover top and sixth from top by Otto Baitz and back cover second from top by Joseph W. Molitor.

Printed in China

Table of Contents

Acknowledgments

We would like to extend special thanks to our clients and advocates, to the individuals and institutions who have given us the opportunity to make exceptional architecture over the years.

All of the people who have been affiliated with our practice, going back to Dick Powell and continuing through to the young architects who work with us today, have given more than might have been expected. Our work also has been strengthened by fine collaborators and consultants.

We would especially like to thank Marika Simms for her skill and care in assembling the materials for this book and Sally Preate Bohlin for her creative and thoughtful contributions to the writing.

A debt is owed to our writers, Joe Esherick, whose friendship and example have always been an inspiration, and Mack Scogin, who extracted his extraordinary sensibilities from Harvard, home, and a busy practice to contribute to this book. Photographers have graciously shared not only their images but their enthusiasm for this project.

Putting the book together has been a pleasurable and satisfying experience, thanks to John Hoke of the AIA Press, Stan Patey and his able staff at Rockport Publishers, and our many friends and associates.

Prologue

This is a time in which belief is often over-whelmed by exponential change. Even in the most serious architectural circles, intellectual games and superficial dogma can take the place of affirmation, and the mediocrity and deadness of much of our environment continue to spread.

Yet, in all of our surroundings there is great richness and power. Belief in the sensuality of place, the emotive qualities of materials, and the ability to give pleasure and insight, to comfort, and to transport, can produce humane and spirited architecture. It is our belief that exceptional architecture comes from the search for solutions which respond to the particular circumstances inherent in each situation.

Increasingly, we have come to see that, in a sense, circumstances are infinite and that working within any one set of habits is too limiting. We must be alive to the subtleties of place, whether manmade or natural; to the varied nature of humans and their particular activities; to the qualities of their institutions; and to the nature of the means with which we build. With both intellect and intuition, we seek solutions that respond to the web of circumstances at hand.

How do we reveal the essence of all things — the sun, the breeze, our hands, the way we move and see and hear, the means with which we make, using stone, metal, wood, glass?

How do we accommodate and gain strength and poignancy from apparent contradictions?

How do we know what to express and what not to express and what manner of truths to reveal?

How do we reflect ourselves, our culture, our past and yet make open-ended places that promise and liberate?

How might we make a place that is so empathic with the surrounding circumstances that it is completed by them?

How might we energize those places where things come together: buildings and situation, here and there, inside and outside, building part and building part, activity and activity?

How do we find the seemingly inevitable answer?

Over the years the interplay of architects within our practice and our responses to more complex and demanding programs and varied environments have broadened our view of the circumstances that affect our work. We are peeling away the layers of our habits and pre-conceptions. We require open-mindedness, willingness, gentleness — a soft, yet no-holds-barred approach.

Peter Q. Bohlin
Bernard J. Cywinski
Jon C. Jackson
Frank W. Grauman
W. Dan Haden, III

Building as Revelation
an essay by Joseph Esherick

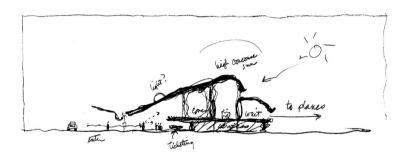

Everything communicates something, but not necessarily the same thing to everyone. Buildings can communicate use, purpose, how they were built. Buildings based on ideologies such as modernism and postmodernism can reveal these ideologies but only insofar as the viewer understands them. If particularities of site, use, and construction further our understanding, if they truly communicate immediate realities, then an imposed ideology or style can only get in the way. Indeed, after the essentials of use and programmatic issues — being sure the building won't fall down or that there are no leaks — are taken care of, the design of buildings today more often is driven by ideology rather than by the particulars of site, use, or construction.

Not everyone has been seduced by style or by the notion of architecture as "scenography." There has emerged a strong group of younger architects who, like poets, work directly and primarily from the realities at hand, who see their role as revealing the nature of immediate circumstance, and who approach their tasks with an openness and a refreshing innocence that goes directly to the point. Such is the work of Bohlin Cywinski Jackson, who, for nearly thirty years, have led this movement. Nothing is private or closed about what they do. Their buildings inform, but not so rigidly as to control. They see the act of building as a revelation, and the role of the architect as one of communicating the nature of the circumstances at hand and conveying how the building got that way.

Why have the traditions of inventive directness, of unelaborated straightforwardness of the innumerable well-known and nameless American designers of the late 19th and early

20th centuries — designers who drew on the immediacies of site, program, and construction technology — so often yielded to design driven by ideology or by the pursuit of identification through an all-too-often arbitrary imagery? Perhaps it has been because, traditionally, one learned about or talked about architecture by looking at buildings or pictures of buildings; it was easy to equate architecture with images and to differentiate them by grouping them into "styles." More likely, design driven by ideology has been market driven, satisfying the need for project identification of either developer, designer, or both. In short, the production of architecture, of buildings, became the production of images; one spoke of classical or modern buildings, often ignoring, especially with modern work, the original, underlying social or cultural purpose.

Buildings were; they were there. They could be imposed on the landscape, and if they didn't fit, one could interpose "landscape architecture" — gardens or built structures — to make the transition. Not so with the work of Bohlin Cywinski Jackson, where buildings are slipped into the landscape as though they had always been there. These architects have not been seduced by arcane ideology, nor have they been tempted to appliqué any wit or humor on the building. What is remarkable is the degree to which they achieve the highest possible technical standards of construction, of energy management, of sophisticated program requirements, and still preserve such freshness and openness. The work of Bohlin Cywinski Jackson has a generosity that is an example to all of us and an openendedness we can all build on. A study of their work is nothing but pleasure.

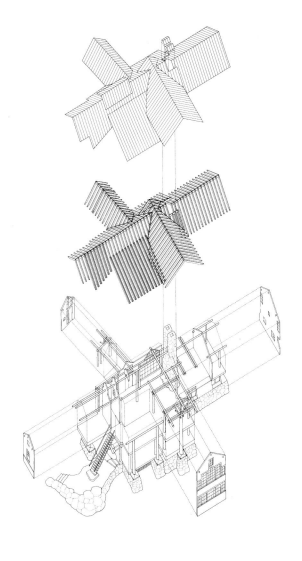

The High Wire
an essay by Mack Scogin

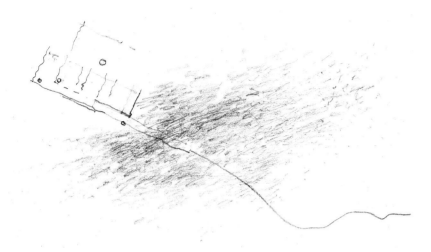

Some years ago I looked carefully at — pondered — what I called the sideways house. It rang with a certain clarity: a refreshing simplicity of form, space, and articulation. At the same time, it touched on the vernacular and rustic without giving way to nostalgia or pastiche. Perhaps it was the industrial sash at the great, culminating corner window of the living space that lent resistance to what could have become a maybe too-sweet cottage. Perhaps there were a number of resistive moves that memory now finds elusive.

I called it the sideways house because of the smart way it presented its narrow elevation to the arrival side and its long elevations to the woods. How good! To slip the house into the forest, perpendicular to the topography, airborne at its extent, the tiniest insertion or intrusion that one would possibly make and still accommodate the program. The entryway along the long side of the house, brushed by the trees, a first physical touch of the forest after arriving in the car, was equally brilliant and simple — a prelude to the living room and the corner window. There was a general, overall sensitivity to site, spareness of the making, and classically strong geometry that transcended the two-dimensional medium of the printed page.

It was clear that the sideways house, for all its simplicity, was not an easy answer to the difficult questions that had been asked, questions that opened gaps for alternative consideration. The picturesque had been held at bay.

Pure humanness was made manifest in the strength and dignity of the house. It was also clear that, with regard to a larger body of work, the sideways house could emerge as a frame for a general question of investment.

It is this general question of investment, that is, at what moment in an architectural investigation can a balance between a deep personal concern for the human condition and the desire to maintain a certain intellectual integrity be achieved, that has most fascinated me about the work of Peter Bohlin, Bernie Cywinski, and their partners over the years. I assume their innate sensibilities toward human physical and psychological potential have been primarily conditioned through their personal histories. Of course, possessing these instincts is one thing, having the confidence and abilities to draw on them for the purposes of an architectural endeavor is another. This humane characteristic of their work is manifest in many, rather obvious ways. The intellectual integrity of their work, however, seems purposely suppressed by what William James referred to as "anti-intellectualist tendencies." This is not to suggest that these architects are not intellectuals — and again I use the James model — but that as intellectuals they tend to argue against rationalist and idealist claims to knowledge. What they do with their architecture is create a mild form of intellectual tease, where rational thought and idealized solutions are at once precisely articulated and cleverly subverted.

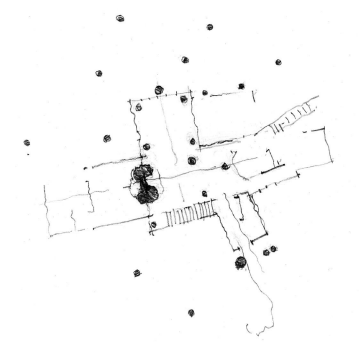

Peter Bohlin's plan sketch of his design for a weekend house in the Adirondacks, for example, proposes another house in a forest. This house is not unlike the sideways house in its basic programmatic intent, but it is totally different in the resolution of the structure's relationship to the nature of its place. However, both houses are definitively modern structures carefully inserted against the forest. The subtle difference is that in the sideways house you go through the forest into the house up against the forest. In the Adirondack House the forest goes through, against, the house you occupy. Of course, the architectural vocabulary of these two houses is naturally quite different. It is difficult for a humanist to build a forest inside a house without using a few trees and boulders.

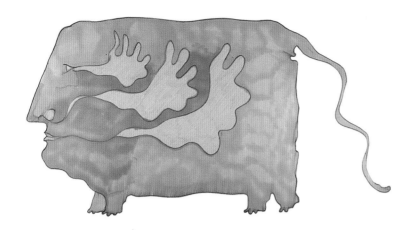

Perhaps one of the first and clearest indications of this tendency toward the intellectual tease can be seen in Peter Bohlin's drawing executed as a young architecture student at Cranbrook Academy of Art in 1960.

At first glance, the figure appears to be a very familiar, specific form — an animal — a bull, or perhaps an elephant. But then you realize that the head or face of the thing is more human, possibly female, or maybe male. But the head is all out of scale with the body of the thing. So are the legs and feet. And what are those odd globs the thing has on its side, or are they inside the thing? Maybe the drawing is actually a section through the he/she or it/thing. No, I've got it, it's one of those things that knows far too much for its own good and it's begun to eat, smell, and see its own ideas. That's it, it's one of those. Or better still, now with the advantage of hindsight, the more important reading of this wonderful drawing is as the portent of an attitude toward a developing personal architecture.

Looking at the work of Bohlin Cywinski Jackson, which spans over twenty years of a productive and diverse practice, one can see this fundamental attitude toward architecture permeating each project in a variety of circumstantial, technical, and stylistic adjustments.

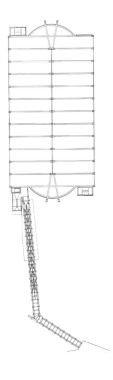

Other circumstantial adjustments to the intellectual tease can be seen in the Irving Avenue Parking Garage at Syracuse University and the Hanover National Bank Branch in Kingston, Pennsylvania.

In the Irving Avenue Parking Garage, Bohlin Cywinski Jackson transform the basic characteristic of an often too-mundane building type by simply recognizing the obvious fact that parking garages are as much about human circulation as automobile circulation. Four critical decisions formulate the transformation: human vertical and horizontal circulation is celebrated at the extremities of the structure, the automobile circulation is expressed in the form of the building, the floor-to-floor heights of the structure are more generous than necessary to accommodate the storage of automobiles, and the structural components of the building are expressed and articulated to enhance their aesthetic value. The result is a remarkable hybrid building, an open-sided, multistory pavilion with contoured floors. A building about transition, in mid-construction or deconstruction, moving from automobile scale to human scale, at once a particular place and a place in between. More importantly, an architecture of transition that elevates the banal activity of parking a car to a distinctive entry experience into the center of the Syracuse University Campus.

The Hanover Bank project is probably the most idiosyncratic of all the Bohlin Cywinski Jackson projects and, for me, is the project most like Peter Bohlin's he/she or it/thing drawing. The building, like the drawing, provokes multiple readings or even can be read as a building meant not to be read. Is it a building in a landscape or is it a landscape that involves some relaxed limitation of enclosed space? And what in the world is that odd hole in the ceiling with potted plants hanging out of it? And what is that red thing? Again, like the he/she or it/thing drawing, there are questions to be answered. But also, like the drawing, the building has a particular charm and pleasantness. It is, I believe, a special place to cash a check in a small town.

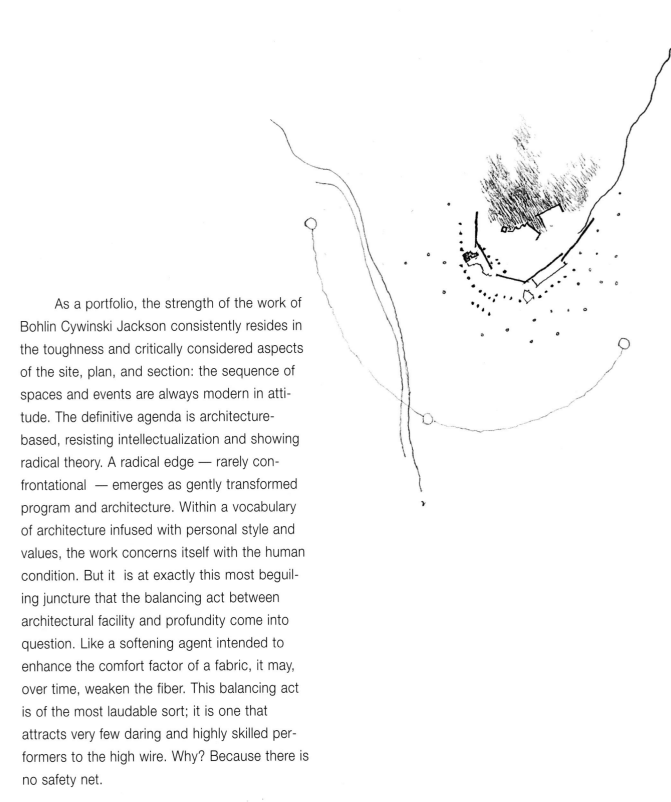

As a portfolio, the strength of the work of Bohlin Cywinski Jackson consistently resides in the toughness and critically considered aspects of the site, plan, and section: the sequence of spaces and events are always modern in attitude. The definitive agenda is architecture-based, resisting intellectualization and showing radical theory. A radical edge — rarely confrontational — emerges as gently transformed program and architecture. Within a vocabulary of architecture infused with personal style and values, the work concerns itself with the human condition. But it is at exactly this most beguiling juncture that the balancing act between architectural facility and profundity come into question. Like a softening agent intended to enhance the comfort factor of a fabric, it may, over time, weaken the fiber. This balancing act is of the most laudable sort; it is one that attracts very few daring and highly skilled performers to the high wire. Why? Because there is no safety net.

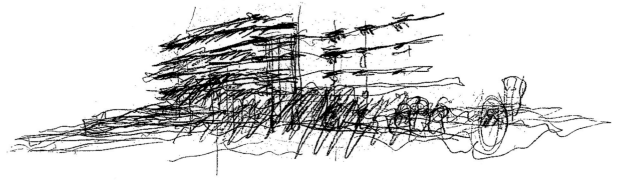

Bohlin Summer House
West Cornwall, Connecticut

This small house was placed on a densely forested hillside at the potent position between dark evergreens and a bright deciduous woodland. Approach, entry, and movement become a rich sequential experience, revealing the subtle transition of the forest: the experience of darkness shifting to liquid patterns of light. Stained green to give it a chameleonlike quality in the forest, the house rests on concrete piers that step through the boulder-strewn landscape. Rather than removing a large granite boulder or moving the building, a telling accommodation was made by scribing a platform to the boulder, anchoring the house in the landscape.

There is great pleasure in modest means: the shimmering green tapestry of the forest seen through red industrial glazing, the poignancy of an operating sash with its subtle gray insect screen floating in the window wall, the rippling profile of an aluminum corrugated roof.

With a keen awareness of the land and the use of simple forms and materials, a place was made which is at once engaging and serene, elegant and comforting.

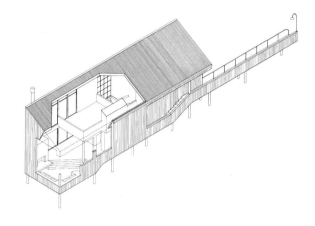

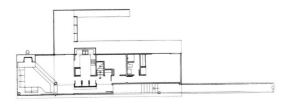

Bohlin Summer House

Gaffney House
Romansville, Pennsylvania

This modest home is located within the remains of an old barn foundation on a farm in Chester County near Philadelphia. The client asked for spaces defined by mood and atmosphere: a sense of openness coupled with privacy, enjoyment of courtyards experienced during a stay abroad, and memories of his childhood on a Midwestern farm. In response to an extraordinary site and an unusual client, the nature of memory and the subconscious were explored. Held free from the original barn walls, the miniature house was given the profile and construction of local farmhouse vernacular.

An angled barn beam supports the second floor between the dining and living spaces permitting a concrete column to extend freely for two stories. The column is placed at the pivot point of a glazed corner of gray blue steel sash facing the courtyard, meadow, and distant forest. Gables are not symmetrical; windows do not quite line up; the plan is slightly skewed to accommodate views to the landscape. Such subtle visual juxtapositions and distortions create a dreamlike ambiance throughout the house, which is both modernist and a simple cottage.

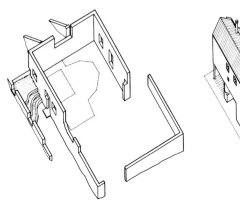

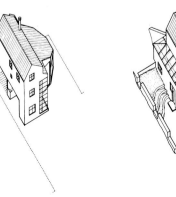

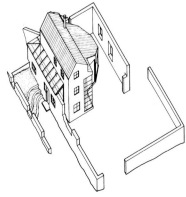

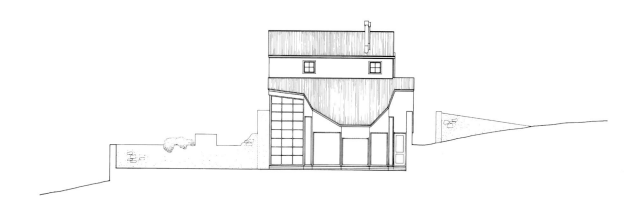

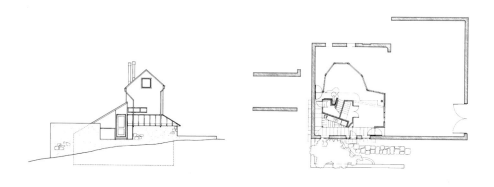

Gaffney House

Gaffney House

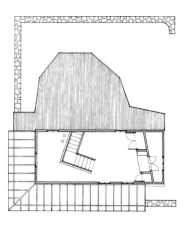

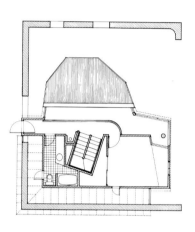

Gaffney House

Weitzman House

Annapolis, Maryland

Located in a mature deciduous forest on a bluff above the Severn River, the house is tightly organized on three levels around a central fireplace and chimney mass. To minimize the encroachment of the house on the forested site, it was designed to rise from a small footprint.

The owners wished to have a home with many of the characteristics of a cottage. Seen from its approach along a winding path, an intimately scaled entry extends out from the building's east wall. The entry contains a stair that climbs up through the house to the third floor. The building's gabled shape and simple windows recall the familiar forms of nearby buildings.

The house is modified by a porch that faces north across the water and is supported by a large, pale yellow tapered column and green-stained truss. The porch is an extension of the three-story bath and kitchen mass, whose interior and exterior windows overlook the river. Throughout the house the surrounding forest and water are seen through a series of glazed interior spaces. Forest light filters down through the interior from a skylight over the central stair.

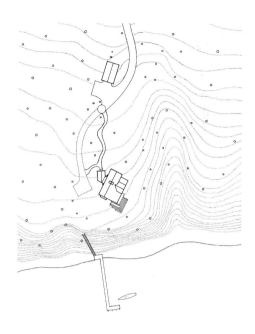

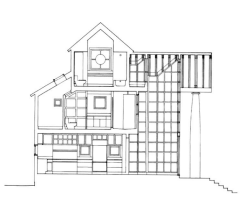

Weitzman House

House in the Adirondacks
New York State

A vacation residence, a separate garage, and a boathouse are arranged on a steeply sloped, forested site at the edge of a mountain lake in upstate New York. The buildings are in the spirit of the Adirondack Great Camps, which, though generally thought of as indigenous, were in fact derived from Japanese and European alpine traditions. The architecture delves into the emotive potential of the materials and the connections between the natural and the manmade.

On approach, roof planes and stone chimneys are visible through pine and hemlock. The slightly angled main entrance on the upper level inflects toward the visitor and is marked by a gable of overscaled logs. The entry leads through a forest of cedar columns toward a massive granite fireplace which rises through the structure and dominates the central living spaces.

Light from high clerestory windows streams down through timber framing into the upper level. Tree columns, red pine bark siding, and rustic stick work engage in a dialogue with the surroundings. The house becomes analogous to the forest, its stone base rising out of the hillside and tree columns extending upward toward a lead-coated copper roof which softly reflects the sky.

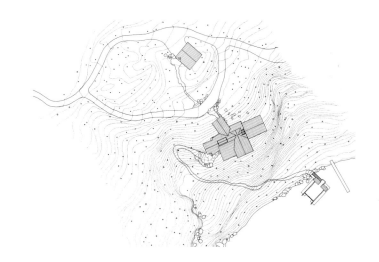

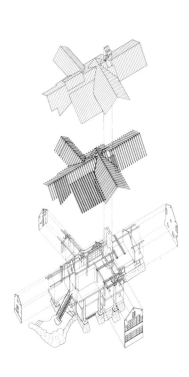

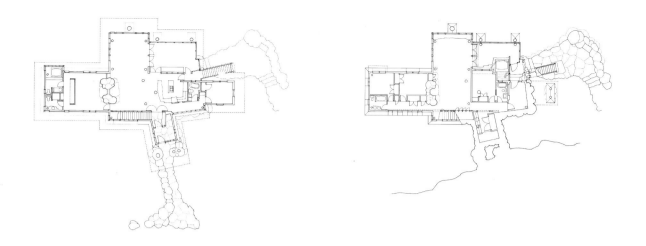

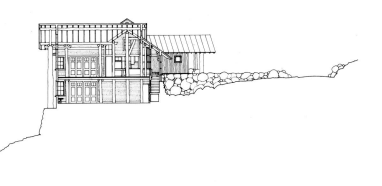

House in the Adirondacks

House in the Adirondacks

Guest House & Garage
Medina, Washington

In order to minimize mass on a narrow waterfront site and reflect the owner's personal style, this residential compound of varied public and private spaces is being slipped into a precipitous hillside. The architecture integrates advanced computer technology with environmental sensitivity.

At the highest point of the property, an earth-covered guest house is invisible on approach and is entered between two concrete walls. Arrival and passage are choreographed to give a sense of moving through the earth, then being released to views of the forest and lake beyond.

Hidden beneath the forest, the garage is approached by driving over it onto a heavy timber trestle that passes its open face. The roof of the twenty-vehicle space is supported by great concrete arches and is broken away to expose the garage's lid which tilts up along the angle of the hillside above. A stone entry court, with a massive, curved, wood retaining wall, leads guests into the reception spaces of the main structure, downslope from the garage.

Materials reveal and express their nature. Concrete, recycled fir, metal, stone, glass, and indigenous landscape reflect the spirit of the Northwest. The buildings are at once modernist and timeless.

This project is a joint venture with James Cutler Architects.

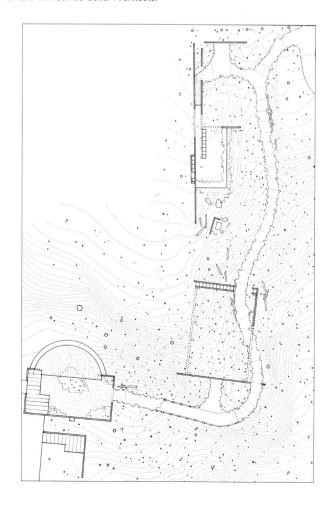

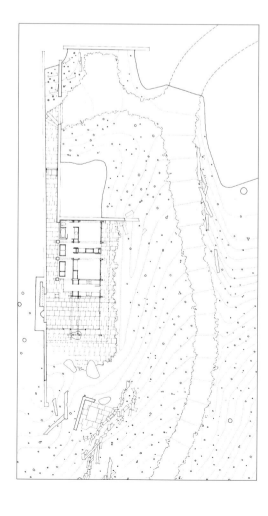

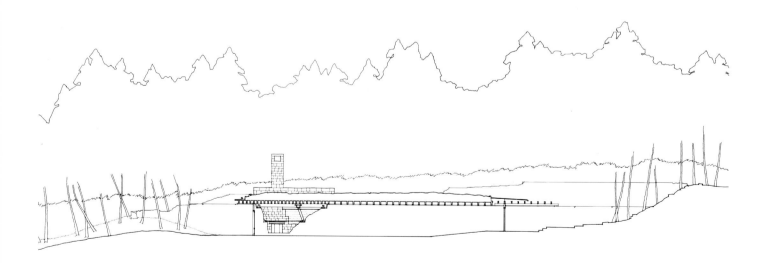

Guest House and Garage

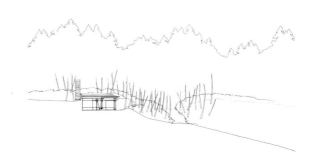

Guest House and Garage

Guest House and Garage

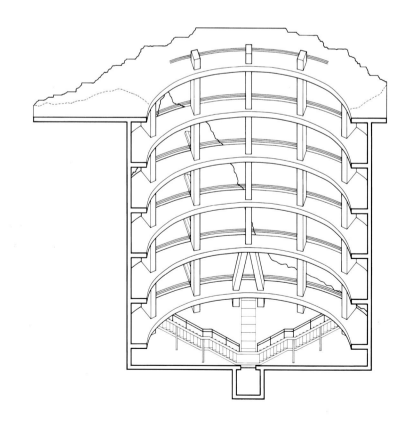

Guest House and Garage

Weekend House
Catoctin Mountains, Maryland

Placed at the edge of a small plateau on a forested mountainside, the house overlooks a stream valley to the south. The man-made cut was the site of an earlier cabin. The clearing's upslope edge is marked by stone ledges and a grove of pine trees.

By employing the logs, heavy timbers, and stonework found in rustic buildings of the early 1900s and arranging the new structure along the south rim of the cut, a remarkably evocative forespace is created. This quarrylike place in the forest speaks of many activities from those of an entry court to a gathering space. On the other side of the extended log wall is a series of loosely arranged sheds that face the sun and overlook the valley and stream below.

The shed roof structures are supported independently of the log walls and detailed with galvanized steel connectors. In the spirit of older camp structures, much of the framing for interior partitions and cabinets, as well as galvanized hardware and electrical fittings, have been exposed to view, adding to the visual richness of the house.

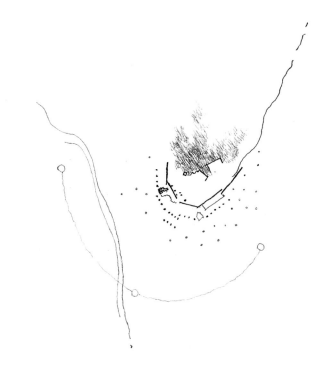

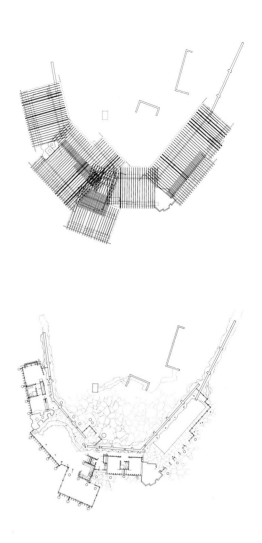

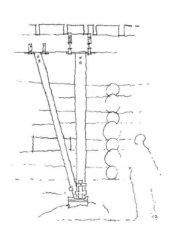

Pool Pavilion
Montgomery County, Pennsylvania

Set in a private arboretum, this indoor pool is connected to a Victorian residential complex that was extensively renovated in the late 1960s, when a greenhouse was added. The pool pavilion is attached to the house by extending the concrete wall of the greenhouse in a series of lively curves.

With its glass skin and articulated aluminum structure, the pavilion is placed at a gentle angle to the residence, opening up views to the sunny landscape. Its glazed roof tilts in two axes to accommodate both the transition from greenhouse to pool and the morphologic ductwork. Three of the pavilion's slender cruciform columns have been removed to accommodate the loosely shaped pool and elongated concrete wall. King post trusses support the resultant longer spans.

In contrast to the delicate structure, an irregularly shaped stone wall encloses the pool's support spaces and extends along its north edge into the landscape, drawing the swimmer's eye to a shaded, fern-filled glen. Technically rigorous yet elusive in spirit, the pool pavilion is both delicate machine and languorous landscape, liquid and stone, reality and illusion.

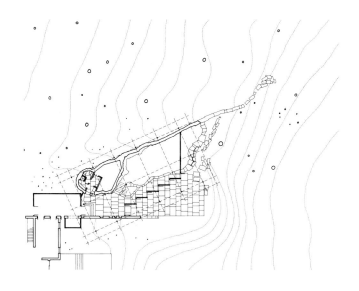

Pool Pavilion

Camp Louise
Columbia County, Pennsylvania

This Girl Scout camp is situated in a narrow valley between two mountain ridges in northeastern Pennsylvania. The camp's central buildings are placed at the forested edge of a field on axis with existing hedgerows that are parallel to the ridges that define the valley.

The dining hall, a great ventilated shed at the south edge of the field, is the camp's largest building. It presents a simple, low-sheltered profile on approach from the central field. Pitching upward away from the field, the dining hall reaches toward the trees and sun. Flaps placed along the entire low northwest face of the dining, kitchen, and serving areas and along the high southeast walls of the building permit cross ventilation. Treelike columns modulate the interior space of the dining hall.

More modest buildings are shaped to their particular uses, and their roofs also tilt upward toward the forest. All structures within the camp were designed to be built by local craftsmen without the use of heavy equipment.

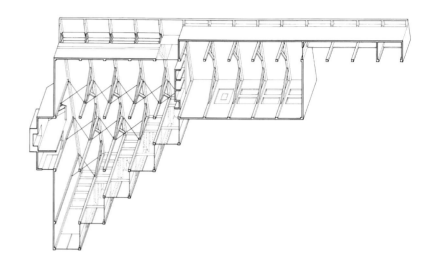

Camp Louise

Shelly Ridge Complex
Miquon, Pennsylvania

This group of buildings translates an urban Girl Scout Council's social and environmental mission into a varied collection of indoor and outdoor places. Adopting the vernacular of an on-site barn and other regional precedents, the architecture is technically rigorous and evocative.

An angled south facing wall alters the program center's basic barn form, gathering and storing the sun's warmth and filtering its light. Research led to the invention of an unconventionally thin thermal wall of timber frame supporting industrial glazing and brick infill panels. The lobby is a semicircular sunspace and functions as a sundial. Devices like the Trombe wall's manually operated awnings and the sundial provide opportunities to understand one's relationship to the natural world.

Gaining richness from its multiple uses and elusive nature, the center's brick stage is also a hearth and a seat for children. Its planes, with their freely curved edges, are like a topographic model or the shale ledges in a Pennsylvania stream.

Along the southern edge of the site, a swimming pool is enclosed by a low wall which becomes one side of a simply constructed bathhouse. The caretaker's house mirrors the program center's gabled facade. Its interior is organized around a wood stove; the hearth is surrounded by four columns in the manner of an aedicula. This project advances passive solar design as a means of place making and expression, and gives children a joyful and optimistic symbol of a more resource-frugal future.

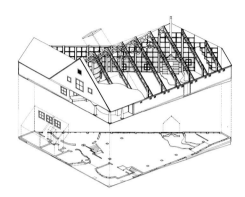

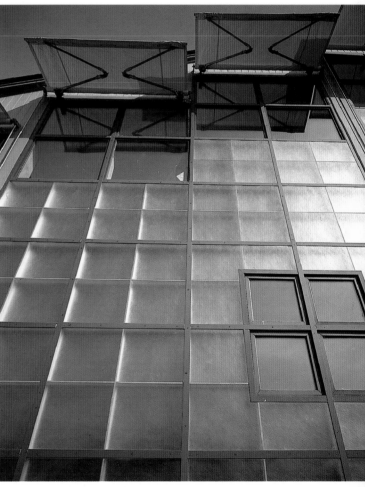

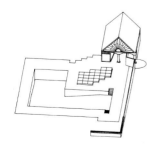

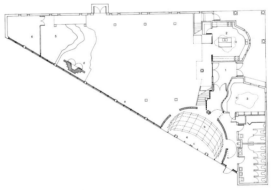

Shelly Ridge Complex

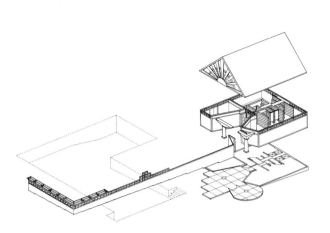

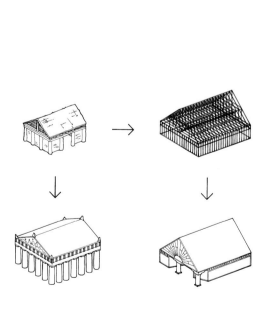

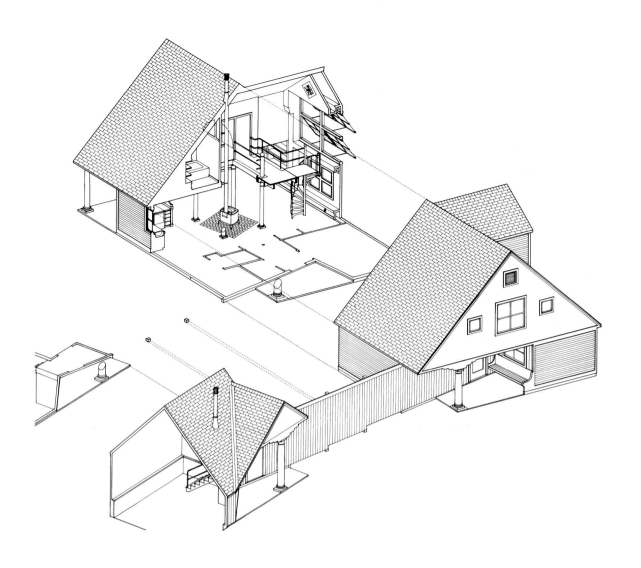

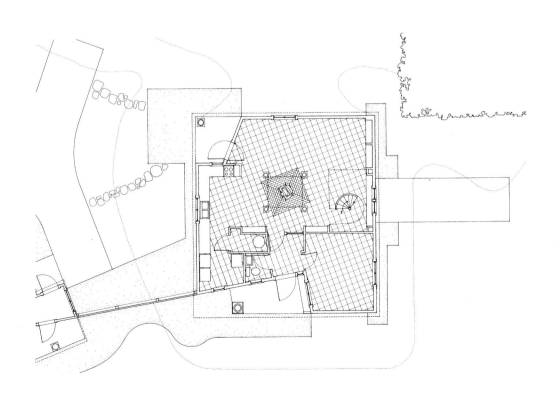

Shelly Ridge Complex

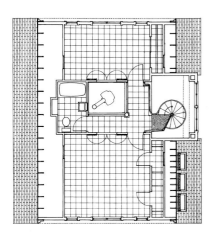

The Winchester Thurston
Lower School
Pittsburgh, Pennsylvania

Winchester Thurston selected a former riding academy as a rural site for their satellite school. When all phases are completed, the school will be an arc of linked segments stepping casually down a slope and around a pond.

Need for speed and economy suggested conventional wood construction. Clear-span wood roof trusses bearing on exterior walls make a simple plan, modified by porches, trellises, and alcoves. Relieved of structural constraints, interior partitions freely accommodate movement through the building. A playful mix of the familiar and the unexpected, the building merges domestic massing with whimsical detailing such as tiny, child-sized windows, monumental columns, and animate shapes cut into exposed framing members.

Enriched meaning and utility are given to necessities: a pair of classroom exits share a common porch to make an informal stage, and shelf brackets become birds and faces.. In the school's lobby, common wood trusses are revealed to create a dynamic interplay with the angled stair below, letting the children see how their school building is made. Expressed means of construction and the interplay of interior and exterior spaces help students relate their classroom experience to the larger world.

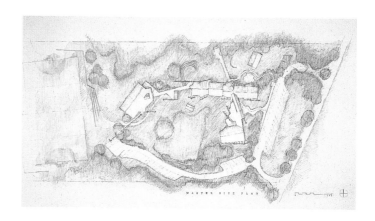

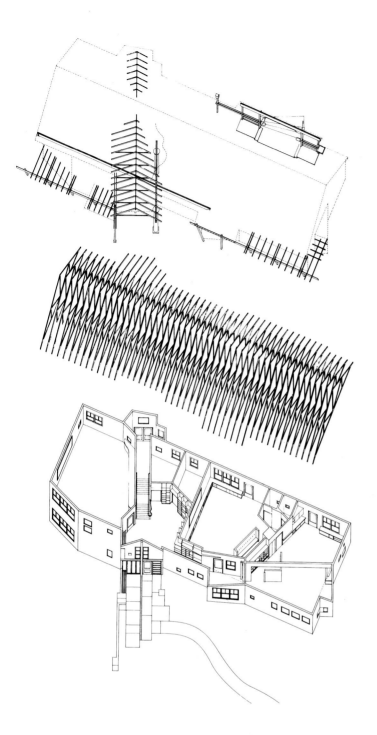

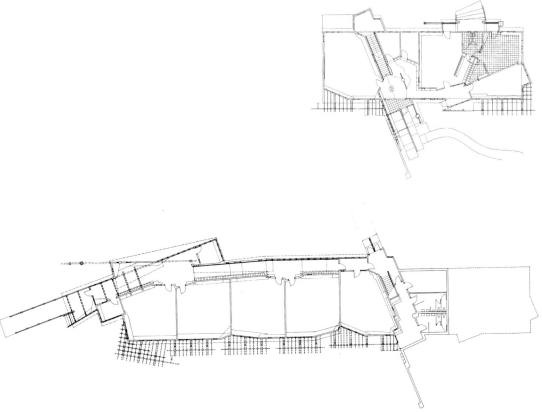

Winchester Thurston

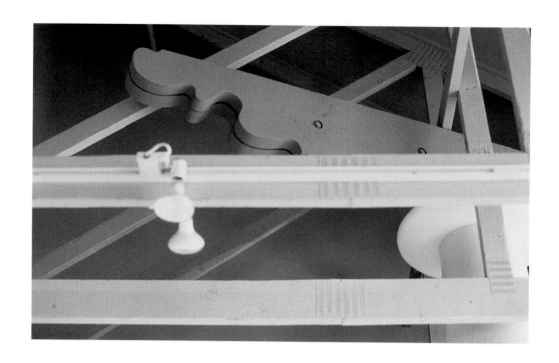

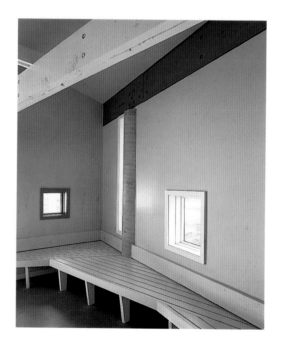

Hanover National Bank
Kingston, Pennsylvania

This banking facility dematerializes into landscape at the corner of a bustling suburban boulevard and a tree-lined residential street. It is a simple brick box modified by a curving glass wall. Vine-covered trellises parallel the streets and step to resolve their irregular geometry.

A cloud-shaped opening in the ceiling beneath a clear skylight reveals ad hoc steel framing and develops an interplay among sky, Arp-like cutout, and everyday construction. The territory of the public space is marked by a sinuous red laminate band that shifts from handrail to check writing surface to purse shelf and back to rail.

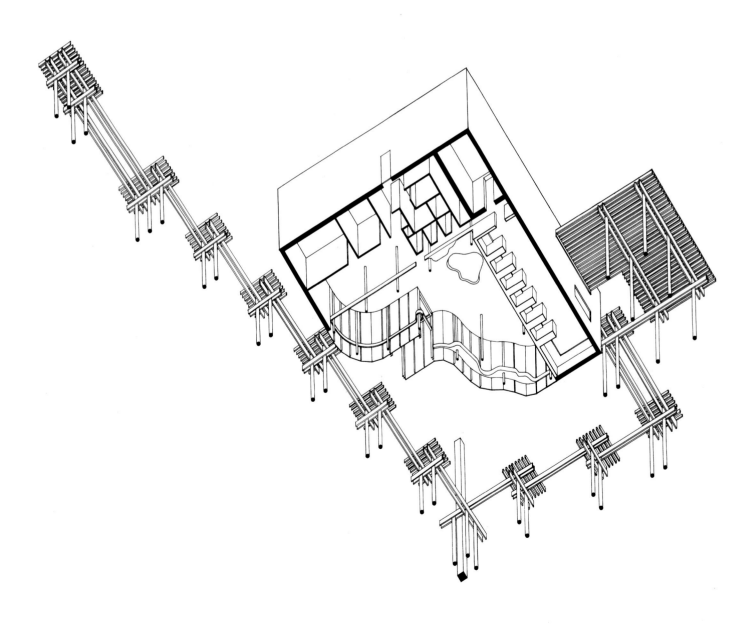

Swimming Center and Playground
Coal Street Park

Wilkes Barre, Pennsylvania

Coal Street Park is a 32-acre municipal park located between two urban neighborhoods on the site of abandoned coal refuse banks. An 800-foot pedestrian mall links the two neighborhoods, connects the various park facilities, and functions as a gathering and exhibit space.

A trellis extending from the mall's entrance plaza to the ice rink separates the play area from the mall. Alternate patterns of progressively challenging play structures engage children of all ages. The rhythms of the trellis and its yellow canvas sun breakers set up a dialogue with the pool's sun breakers across the mall.

Covered with an air-supported fabric structure during cold weather, the swimming center was designed to function year-round. Mechanical equipment pods that heat and pressurize the dome were located on the roof of the linear bath-house. Large ducts reach down from the pods to supply air to the aquadome.

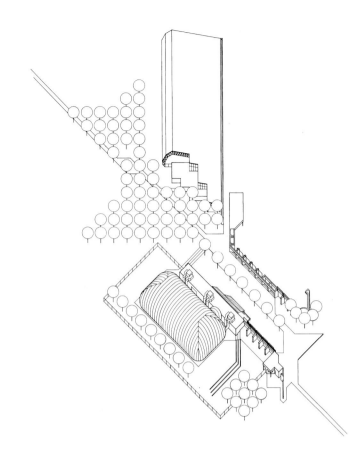

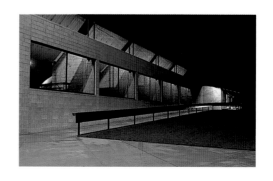

Ice Rink
Coal Street Park
Wilkes Barre, Pennsylvania

The ice rink has the tough mechanistic quality of industrial steel sheds of the late 19th and early 20th centuries. The 85 by 200 foot rink is positioned to permit circulation along its south side nearest the park's pedestrian spine. The roof pitches up toward the north, supported by steel pipe trusses that break over to the ground on the north side. The ribbed aluminum roof deflects the sun's heat and is an effective light reflector for the interior. Sloping upward from the south, the structure shades the ice but does not overpower the nearby modestly scaled play areas. The interplay of the symmetrical rink and its asymmetrical roof gives the skating shed a dynamic presence.

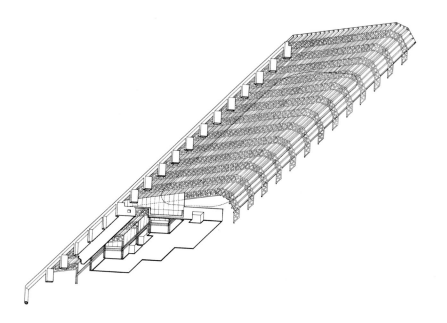

Harrisburg
Airport Terminal
Middletown, Pennsylvania

Conceived as the gateway to the state capital, this international air terminal binds symbol, ceremony, and utility.

The building's airfoil shape suggests flight and reflects the traveler's path from ground transportation to gate. Reminiscent of traditional railroad station design, broad, airy concourses and open waiting areas are housed under one great roof. Its light-filled spaces are liberating, as if one were moving in a region between flight and everyday life. A large eyebrow window illuminates the central stairway and escalators, and clerestories fill the length of the upper concourse with natural light.

Accommodating the movement of passengers and services, the terminal's transverse section produces a building that orients the public and is easy to use. Its minimal depth shortens travel distance between plane and curb. The ground-level concourse along the roadway serves all ticketing and baggage functions, while the upper level concourse provides direct enclosed access to aircraft and passenger services.

The terminal is both a spirited building and a direct response to functional necessities. Its repetitive linear pattern facilitates future growth.

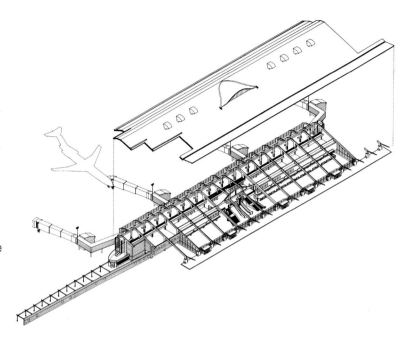

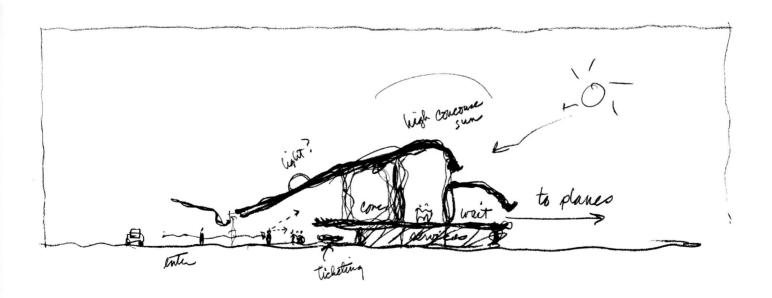

Harrisburg Airport Terminal

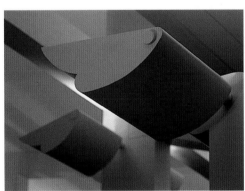

Knott Center
Mount Saint Mary's College
Emmitsburg, Maryland

A linear galleria links arena, fieldhouse, pool, and other program spaces, making it the key architectural element of this athletic, recreation, and convocation center. The building is visually connected to the main academic campus across a major roadway by the common axis of its concourse, the college's principal quadrangle, and the spire of DuBois Hall, Mount Saint Mary's symbol.

Each major space flanking the central galleria employs its own structural means to accommodate its particular use. Triangulated steel truss arches span the fieldhouse, supporting a fabric roof that transmits daylight into the space. The roof becomes a lantern by night, visible from car and campus.

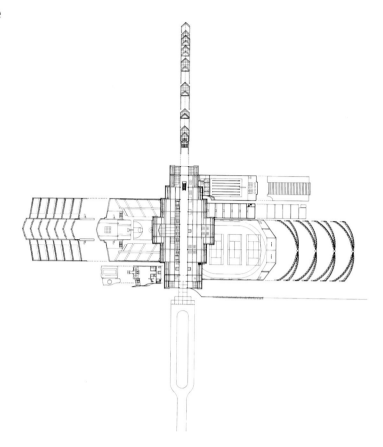

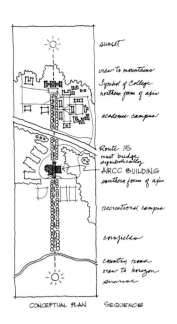

CONCEPTUAL PLAN SEQUENCE

sunset

view to mountains
Symbol of College
northern focus of axis

academic campus

Route 15
must bridge
symbolically
ARCC BUILDING
southern focus of axis

recreational campus

cornfields

country road
view to horizon
sunrise

Bensalem
Municipal Building

Bensalem, Pennsylvania

A long, low wall in the landscape is broken at its change in axis by a glass entry pavilion to reveal a garden. Conveying an understated civic presence, the wall parallels the 600-foot length of the entrance road and screens police and township administration activities which are housed in rectangular brick masses that flank the glazed entrance. The communal council chamber rises up behind the horizontal forms, announcing its role as the ceremonial center of this public building.

Slender steel columns support interior beams that become vine-covered trellises, and slate paving slides from interior to exterior, fusing building and landscape.

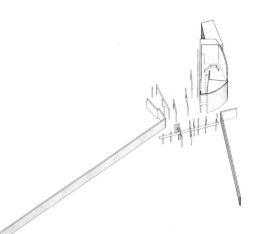

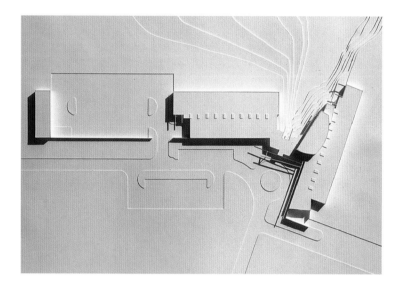

Bucks County Free Library
Doylestown, Pennsylvania

The library joins the extraordinary Mercer Museum of 1915 and the Addison Hutton prison of 1885, now part of the new James A. Michener Art Museum, in an orthogonal relationship to the street common to all three structures. The library's mass sets up the boundary of a new quadrangle which will be developed by future buildings for performance and exhibition.

A tall gabled spine organizes the library. Natural light fills the expansive reading rooms and library services areas, and at night the continuous clerestory and glazed ends of the spine glow in the landscape. Reminiscent of ennobled rural building types, the library is a graceful addition to this evolving historic site and circumstance.

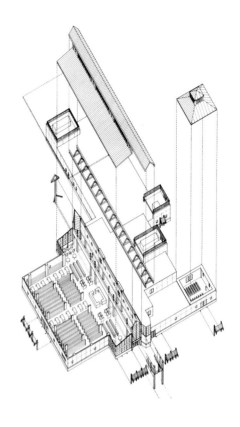

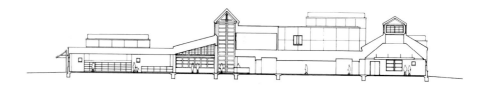

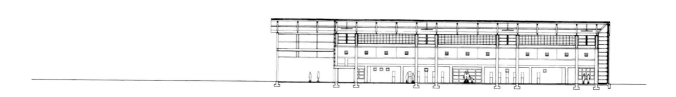

Bucks County Free Library

InterMetro Industries Headquarters
Wilkes-Barre, Pennsylvania

The George W. Guthrie School was built in 1914-15 using the most innovative construction methods of the day. Although abandoned in the early 1970s, the architects found that rehabilitation of the building as a corporate headquarters presented significant economic, aesthetic, and functional advantages over new construction and were able to shepherd its nomination to the National Register of Historic Places.

In accord with the building's landmark status, the exterior was restored and a new entrance was made at the rear facade. Framed by a masonry and steel armature placed in the center bay, this entrance establishes a new axis and orientation for the building. Through the use of glazed interior partitions and sloped interior clerestories, the building is infused with natural light borrowed from the large steel stairwell windows and existing skylights in the hipped roof.

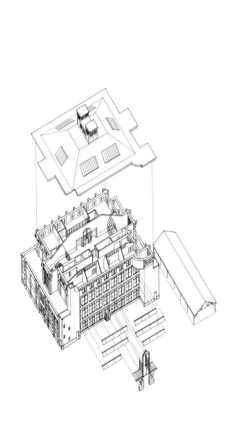

Software Engineering Institute
Carnegie Mellon University
Pittsburgh, Pennsylvania

Carnegie Mellon University's Software Engineering Institute symbolizes Pittsburgh's metamorphosis from an industrial giant to a research-led economy. In the heart of a precinct of monumental buildings, the site faces the limestone spires of St. Paul's Cathedral immediately across a broad avenue and the neoclassical Mellon Institute to the west. The building empathizes with its neighbors while standing as a powerful symbol of the future.

The SEI's Fifth Avenue face is aligned with the Institute's oblique facade; its granite podium, limestone cladding, and glazing reflect the Institute's colonnades, entablatures, and podium. Recognition of St. Paul's positions the primary entrance to the SEI, which is placed on axis with the nave of the neo-Gothic cathedral. SEI's limestone entry pavilion reflects the vertical massing and materials of the church, as the Institute's semicircular forespace is a counterpoint to its intricately detailed exterior.

The building resonates with its surroundings while providing a workplace that accommodates the development of rapidly advancing software technology. Accessible cable trays and integrated lighting in bracketed beams give character to the building's circulation spaces and represent the lifeblood of the facility.

This project was a joint venture with Burt Hill Kosar Rittelmann Associates.

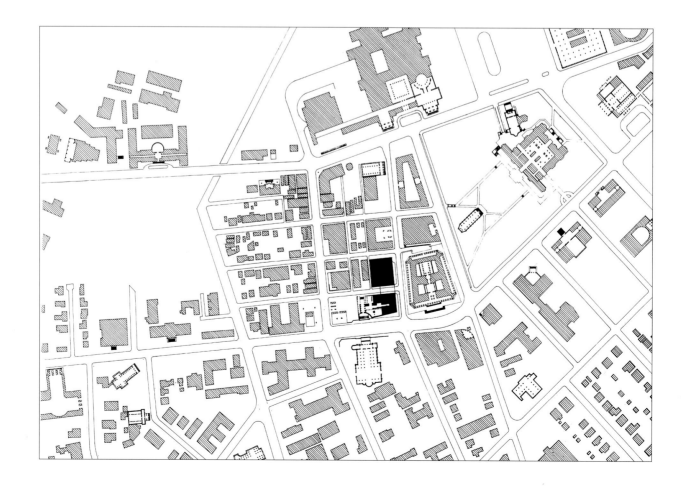

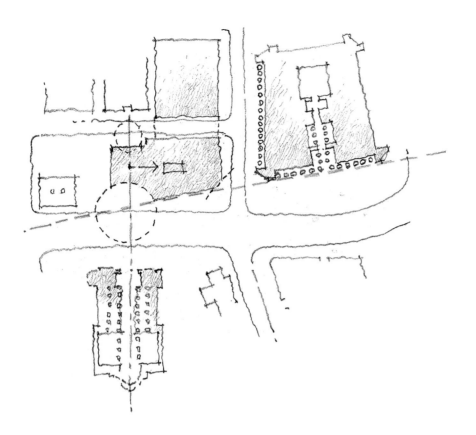

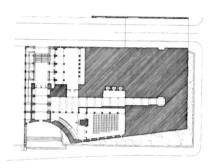

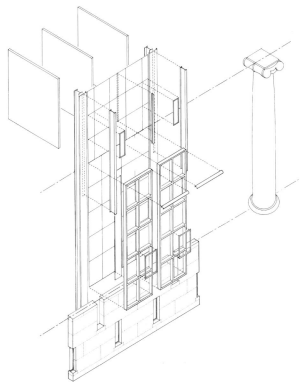

Software Engineering Institute

113

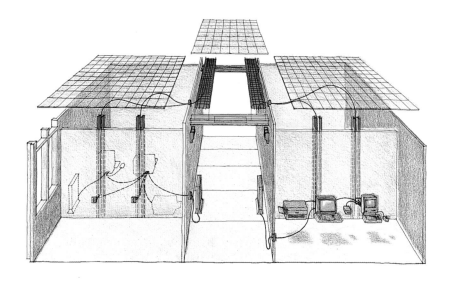

The Maxwell School
Syracuse University
Syracuse, New York

Master Plan: Having attained a sense of destiny by the early part of this century, Syracuse University engaged in a search for a formal campus plan and ultimately committed to a classical design proposed by John Russell Pope. The new master plan reaffirmed Pope's original intention and identified expansion opportunities. Eggers Hall, added at the historic campus center, would re-establish the spatial ordering system initiated in the 1920s, and two new formal campus spaces would emerge: one fronted by the Maxwell School and another centering on Hendricks Hall, Pope's domed chapel.

Eggers Hall, The Maxwell School Expansion: Eggers Hall triples the size of the Maxwell School, encompassing its well-known Master of Public Administration program and all of the University's social science departments. The new building responds to the contemporary role of technology in the academic environment, incorporating a full spectrum of media, communication, and computing capabilities.

The school requested that the buildings reinforce their sense of community by creating an environment conducive to collegial interaction. Communal spaces link diverse research and instructional environments, and two skylit atria provide focus and light at the heart of this large building. The western atrium commons links Eggers Hall to old Maxwell and becomes the grand public room of the complex.

While designed to evolve with the university's commitment to advanced information technology, Eggers Hall becomes the architectural link between Pope's two Georgian buildings. Adopting the mathematical relationships of classical proportions, Eggers Hall's massing and details are rooted in past, present, and future.

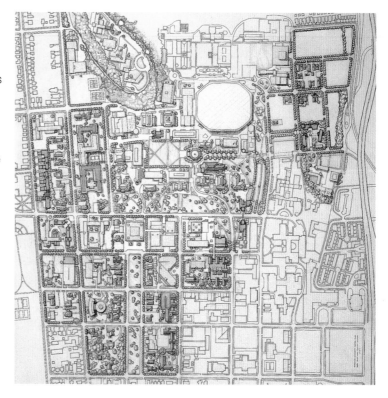

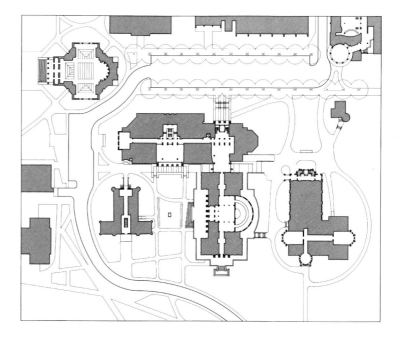

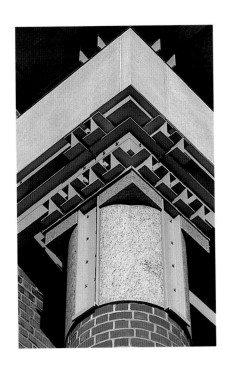

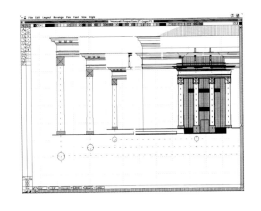

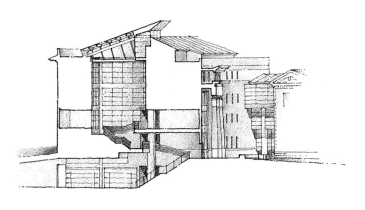

Science Building and Townhouses
St. Mary's College of Maryland

St. Mary's City, Maryland

The expanded north campus of St. Mary's College adjoins the site of Maryland's original colonial settlement, and in the tradition of the great academic campuses, takes its character from the indigenous architecture of the region. The new science building facility adopts the plain language of the colony's Wren-inspired Assembly Building. Its paired brick chimneys recall the region's historic manor houses and function as laboratory fume exhaust stacks. A series of outdoor rooms, human scale, and windows for all interior spaces are achieved by breaking the mass into wings.

The student townhouses are arranged in a crescent wrapping around a running track. The building is positioned on axis with the playing field and track, its head is aligned with the science facility's central passageway, and chimneys flank a major portal to the adjacent commons. Removed from other buildings and dense human activity, the tail of the crescent is made more delicate and graceful, as if slipping into neighboring fields. A real and memorable place has been made by the spirited combination of architectural precedent and programmatic response.

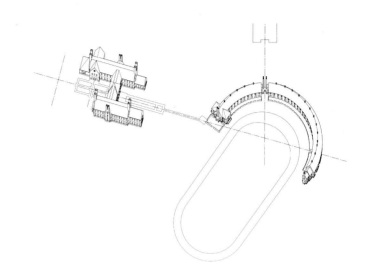

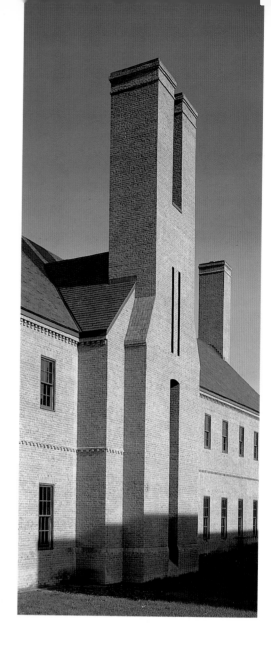

St. Mary's College

Irving Avenue Garage
Syracuse University

Syracuse, New York

This parking garage expresses the essential nature of its various elements, including its structure and use, relying upon this expression for its architectural strength.

The ends of the garage, which front onto streets, are curved and open, accommodating the turns of the interior driving loop. To minimize cracking and the intrusion of corrosive road salts brought on by severe winters in the 433-car facility, computer modeling was used to individually design each column-beam for zero tension stress. The ends of the post-tensioned beams are capped for protection from the elements, as are the roof deck columns which stub up in anticipation of future vertical expansion.

An atypical openness is established by the use of cable restraints and by the greater than normal floor-to-floor dimension. The resulting benefits of natural light in the daytime and transparency at night do much to dispel the vulnerability people often feel in structured parking facilities. The increased floor height also accommodates the sloped site, providing the elevation required for the pedestrian bridge to connect the garage comfortably to the hilltop campus core. Transparency and forthright expression convert a utilitarian building into a worthy gateway to the university campus.

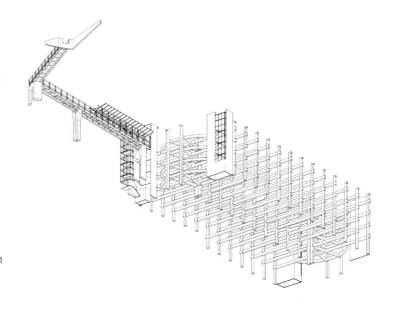

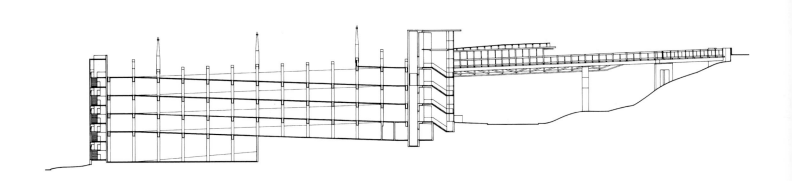

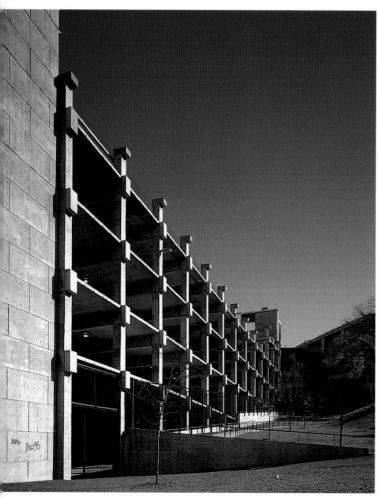

Irving Avenue Garage

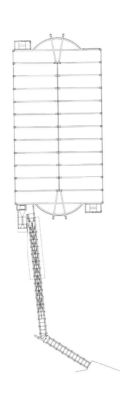

Biotechnology Center
University of Pittsburgh
Pittsburgh, Pennsylvania

The University of Pittsburgh's Center for Biotechnology and Bioengineering is the first building in the Pittsburgh Technology Center, developed above the remains of steel rolling mills along the Monongahela River. The long, narrow site suggested a pattern of linear buildings broken by hedgerows of trees for entrance and service access.

Most of the structure is programmed for wet laboratories wrapped around a dense mechanical backbone that permits a variety of future configurations. The first floor is devoted to laboratory support functions and a multistoried stair hall leads visitors up and through public spaces to magnificent views of the river and distant cityscape. Floating within the narrow atrium, informal meeting places adjacent to each floor of laboratories foster the interactive spirit of research.

Master plan design guidelines, program requirements, and site conditions shape the building's exterior. The north entry face is composed of taut steel panels with flush joinery. In contrast, the corrugated metal panels, applied sun screens, structural framework, and varied angles of the southern facade heighten the play of light and evidence the particular functions within. The building represents sophisticated technology while alluding to industrial antecedents.

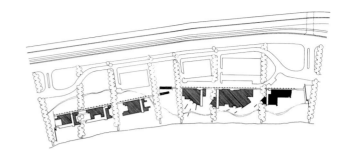

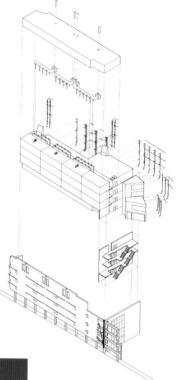

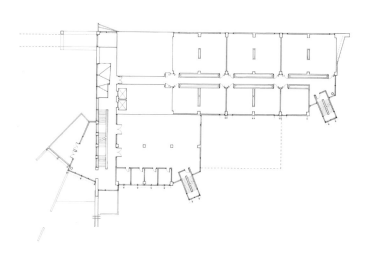

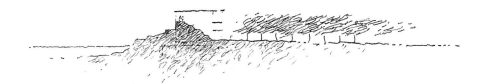

Biotechnology Center

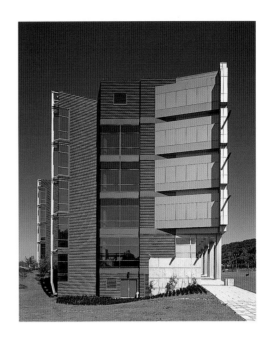

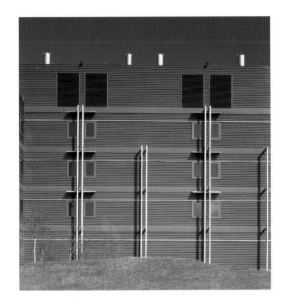

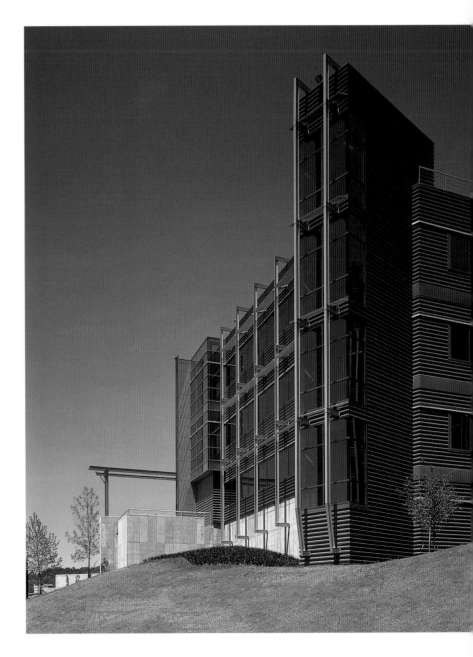

Biotechnology Center

Pennsylvania Higher Education Assistance Agency

Harrisburg, Pennsylvania

A seven-story blue masonry wall divides this 375,000 square-foot office building into two distinct masses. A highly articulated fronthouse faces the street and contains public-oriented facilities; the backhouse is made up of expansive loft spaces that can be subdivided to accommodate changing departmental activities.

Entry and circulation occur along the 400-foot length of the wall, which slices through the building into the landscape. The wall reinforces the low, elongated profile of the building — a tower turned on its side in response to the shape of its site.

PHEAA's fronthouse communicates its public nature through the use of structurally expressive canopies and clearly defined lobbies and circulation patterns. Articulated structure, indented wall planes, and a delicate roof overhang reduce its scale. The backhouse loft space is wrapped in a tight glass skin. A tier of dark skeletal bridges link the office building to an adjacent, unadorned concrete parking garage.

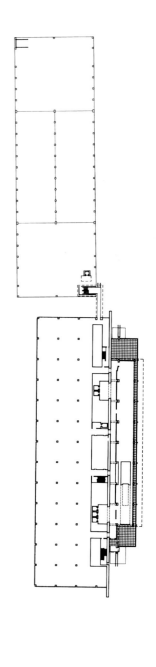

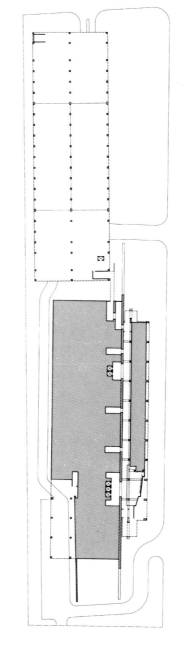

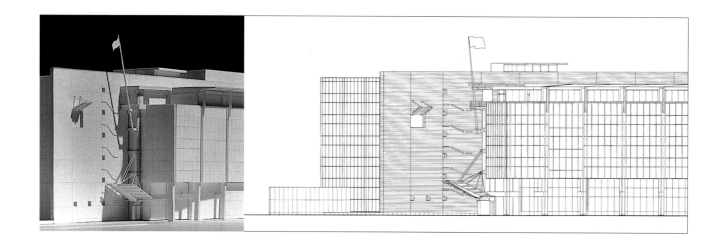

PENNSYLVANIA HIGHER EDUCATION ASSISTANCE AGENCY   1200

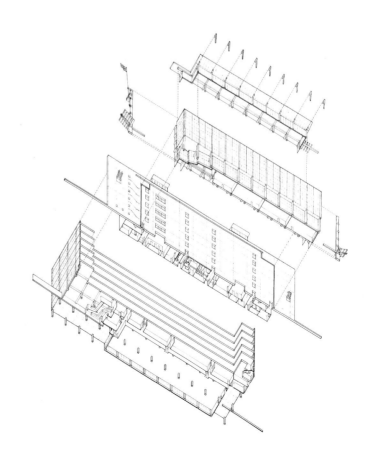

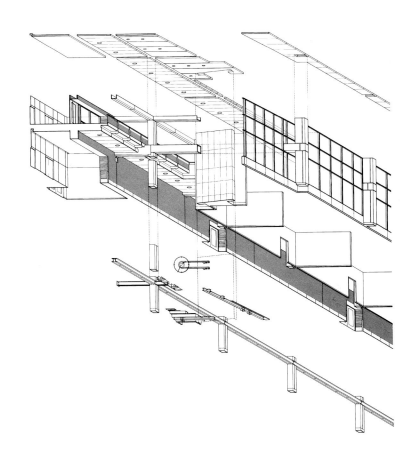

The Intelligent Workplace
Carnegie Mellon University
Pittsburgh, Pennsylvania

The Intelligent Workplace at the Center for Building Performance & Diagnostics is a long-term demonstration, research, and teaching project for the Advanced Building Systems Integration Consortium. The project's design is the result of a collaboration with Swiss architect Pierre Zoelly and the research staff at the Center. The structure, a rooftop extension of Margaret Morrison Carnegie Hall, will enable demonstrations of innovations in building enclosure, interior, HVAC, and telecommunications systems.

By breaking the massing of the structure into a series of modular bays, the roof form both maximizes solar performance and creates a scale sympathetic with the rhythms of the terra-cotta facade below. The interior is planned as a village that encourages interaction while retaining areas for greater individual privacy. The users are served by a highly integrated building systems chassis which is flexibly designed for future investigation.

As a lived-in office, research, and educational environment, the Intelligent Workplace will provide a test bed for assessing the performance of new processes and products.

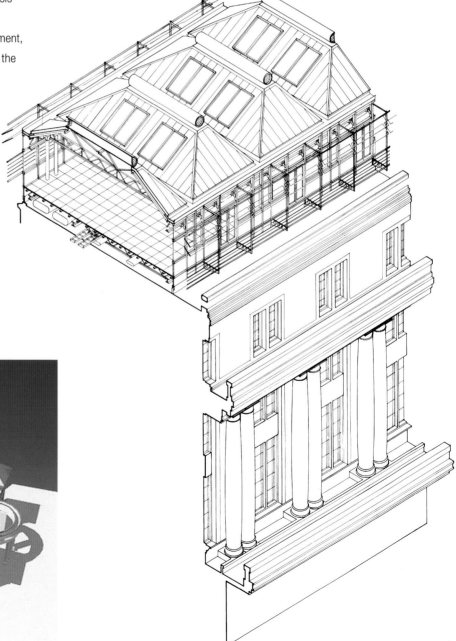

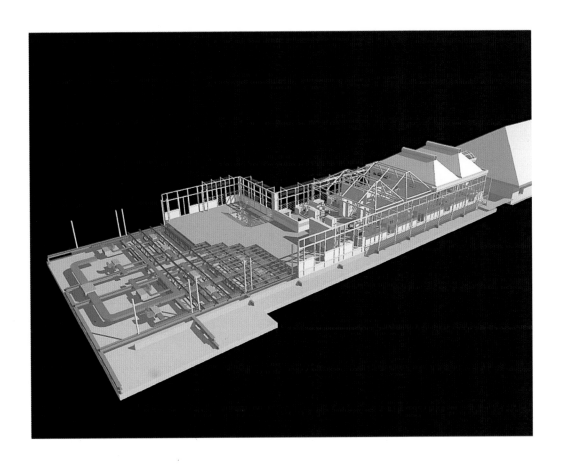

Sigma Xi – The Scientific Research Society

Research Triangle Park, North Carolina

Sigma Xi, The Scientific Research Society, selected a site in North Carolina's Research Triangle Park for the Society's international headquarters and scholars' center. Here multidisciplinary teams of distinguished researchers will bring scientific insights to the interaction of technology and public policy issues. Reflecting Sigma Xi's vision, the design is at once technologically advanced and intimately connected to the natural world.

Headquarters functions are located in a linear building set counter to the sloping woodland, and its southern face is shaded by light vine-covered metal armatures. Scholars' spaces are arranged in two earth-covered wings cut into the descending landscape. All of the building's elements come together in a great airy room for gathering and dining.

As one approaches, only the lyrical metal roof floating over the central space is visible above the landscape. Entry is choreographed as a sequence of discovery; it is a subterranean passage, an arrival in the heart of the center, which opens out to the forest beyond.

APPROACH –

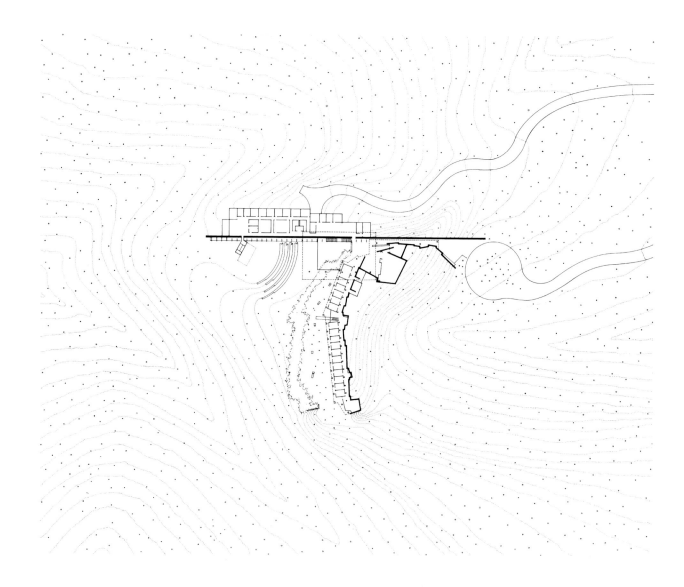

APPROACH   /DISCOVERY-MYSTER)   RELEASE

AMPHITHEATRE

Wilkes-Barre Downtown
Wilkes-Barre, Pennsylvania

Following the Hurricane Agnes Flood in 1972, the architects were asked to help reconstitute Wilkes-Barre's Public Square and South Main Street, the city's principal commercial thoroughfare.

A glazed 1800-foot-long canopy extends along the storefronts on the west side of Public Square and the first block of South Main Street, providing shelter from the elements while unifying the downtown. Designed as a shed, the canopy pitches up to a point several inches from the existing building faces. Its rafters cantilever from a continuous triangulated steel pipe truss supported on pipe columns. The system's muscle, a dark-red pipe truss, ties the shopping district together, adjusting to the varying circumstances along the edges of the square and street and crossing South Main Street at mid-block.

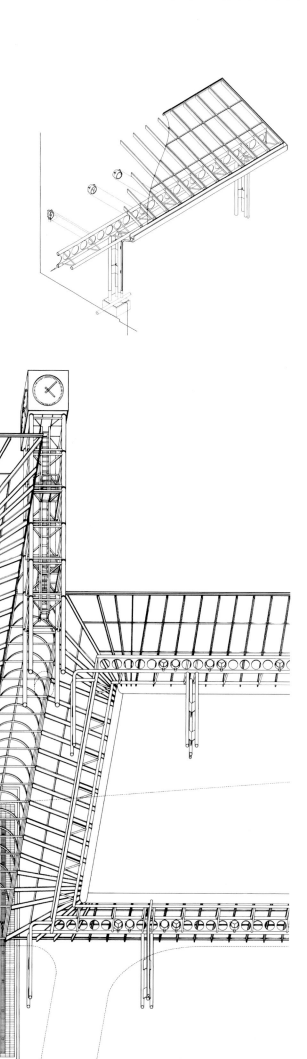

Wilkes-Barre Public Square
Wilkes-Barre, Pennsylvania

Public Square, the psychological and historical center of the city, is both a passive green space and a great outdoor room for activities such as festivals and a weekly farmers' market. Set diagonally in the downtown street grid, the square has asymmetrical aspects even as it maintains its centering quality. It incorporates seating, an amphitheater, fountains, and children's play areas.

Retaining the square's original crossed-path pattern, the perimeter was enlarged to incorporate a ring of cherry trees in raised granite planters that function as traffic buffers, additional seating, and stalls for farmers' market vehicles. A band of granite pavers flows around the square, its patterns deforming to accommodate the various new and existing elements. Petroglyphs sandblasted in the paving blocks are magic marks of natural phenomena, the region, society, and the architects' personal allusions.

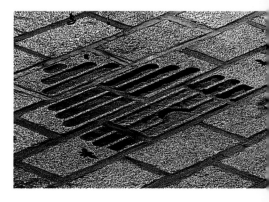

Ritter Park
Huntington, West Virginia

Ritter Park is an early twentieth century urban park conceived in the romantic landscape tradition.

Its playground was designed to occupy a grassy basin,
once a pond, rimmed with hemlock and spruce — a mysterious
place in the landscape. Separate play structures provide a variety
of spatial and kinesthetic experiences; their forms knit together in a
network of relationships that are revealed in the course of play. An
area for the smallest children rests in the sloping bank of the basin
below a stand of evergreens. A curved linear array of places and
objects is made of stone cubes whose simple shapes suggest toy
building blocks or ancient ruins.

Selection and placement of plants, structures, and path-
ways for the Ritter Rose Garden support expanded interpretive
missions while heightening the romantic qualities that link the
garden to the rest of the park. Roses are grouped to create a
series of outdoor rooms, each with its own character. A pavilion of
open lathing, supported by steel caryatids, provides visual focus
and shade for the garden.

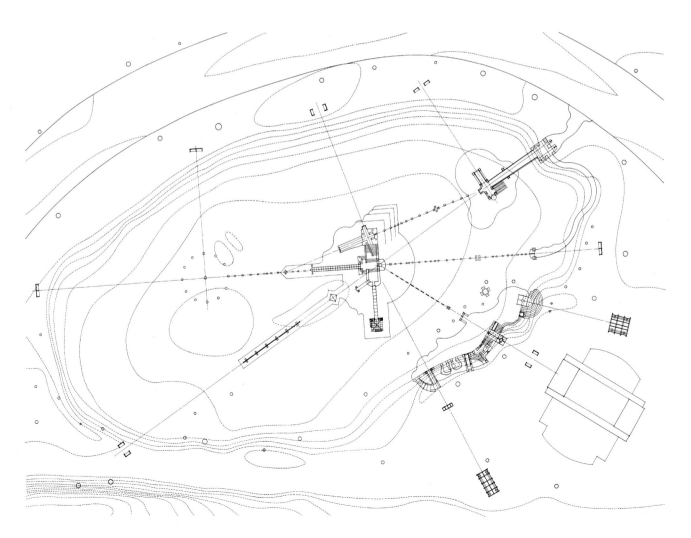

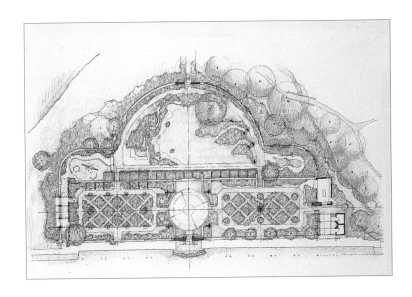

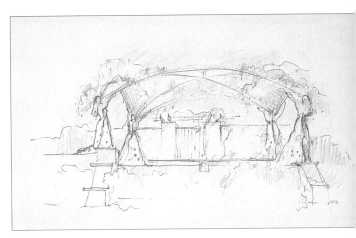

Great Falls Historic District
Paterson, New Jersey

Founded by Alexander Hamilton at the Passaic River's Great Falls, Paterson, New Jersey, was the nation's first planned industrial center.

In the urban design and public improvement plan for the Great Falls Historic District, prototypical designs for exterior rehabilitation of buildings along the commercial streets were developed. The program focused on improving public amenities, parks, and streetscapes to encourage private restoration of historic mill structures.

The Great Falls District had lacked street lighting and similar public amenities during its industrial heyday, and since the commercially available reproductions were not appropriate, a versatile street furniture system was designed. Using a minimal number of parts, custom cast-iron connector elements and escutcheons were combined with standard steel pipe sections. While clearly made and installed in the 1980s, the system conveys the toughness of 19th Century industrial artifacts.

Master Plan
Philadelphia Zoological Garden

Philadelphia, Pennsylvania

During a decade of collaboration, the architects and The Zoological Society of Philadelphia developed a master plan and a design manual to guide the future growth and conservation of the Philadelphia Zoological Garden. These guidelines were first realized in the improvement of the main thoroughfare, where the paving, lighting standards, and railings were inspired by the Zoo's inhabitants and Victorian precedent, dating back to the founding of the society.

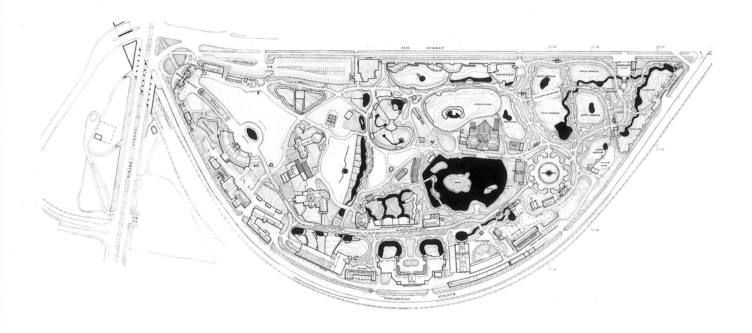

Carnivore Exhibits
Philadelphia Zoological Garden
Philadelphia, Pennsylvania

The perceived environment has been manipulated to cause the visitor to experience the excitement, danger, fascination, and pleasure of direct participation in the animal's world. Radiant light pierces grotto-like space as ethereal steel armatures rise out of the landscape, their steel mesh enclosures containing the more dangerous carnivores. Labyrinthine paths through condensed theatrical contrasts of closure and expansiveness, dark and light, giant boulders and gentle glades lead to intimate views of the most benign and most ferocious animals through fissures and gaps in the rocks and rolling vistas.

Philadelphia Zoological Garden

Zig Zag Wren House
and Stan's Bird Dial

Based on a traditional four-square wren house, this structure is carefully shaped to the size and proportions of its inhabitants. The design extends the house to the ground in a zig-zag that discourages climbing predators and achieves the nine-foot height preferred by the birds. The wren house was exhibited at the Parrish Art Museum and sold at auction for the benefit of the museum.

Stan's bird dial was a birthday gift for a friend. It is both a birdhouse and a sundial, employing stainless steel, wood, and a moss garden.

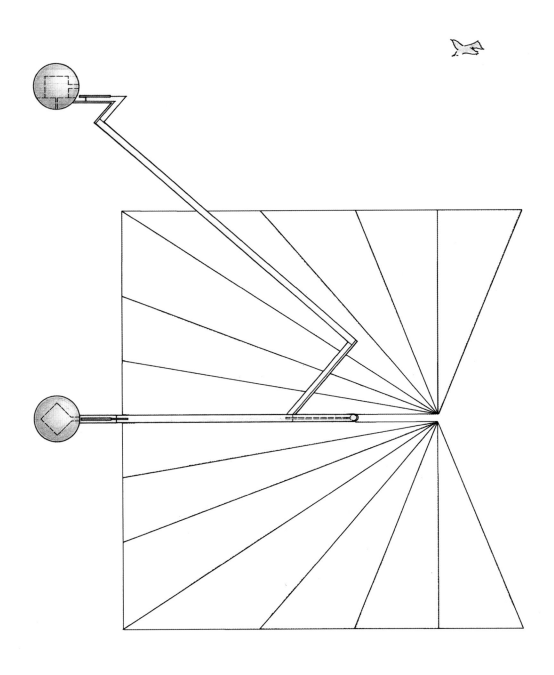

Chronology

House

Location: Bear Creek, Pennsylvania
Client: Mr. and Mrs. Eric Q. Bohlin
Dates: 1965-1966

Factory and Offices

Location: Mountaintop, Pennsylvania
Client: Fagersta Steels Incorporated
Dates: 1967-1969

House

Location: Shavertown, Pennsylvania
Client: Mr. and Mrs. Edward Schechter
Dates: 1968-1969

House Renovation and Addition

Location: West Dallas, Pennsylvania
Client: Mr. and Mrs. Stanley Davies
Dates: 1969-1970

Camp Louise

Location: Columbia County, Pennsylvania
Client: Penn's Woods Girl Scout Council
Dates: 1969-1972

House

Location: Erie, Pennsylvania
Client: Mr. and Mrs. Paul Skala
Dates: 1970-1971

Coal Street Park Swimming Center
Location: Wilkes-Barre, Pennsylvania
Client: Wilkes-Barre Board of Recreation
Dates: 1970-1972

Coal Street Park Playground
Location: Wilkes-Barre, Pennsylvania
Client: Wilkes-Barre Board of Recreation
Dates: 1971-1973

Branch Office
Location: Kingston, Pennsylvania
Client: Hanover National Bank
Dates: 1972-1974

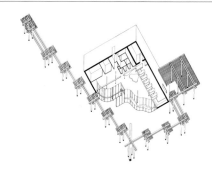

Office Building
Location: Randolph Township, New Jersey
Client: Westinghouse Electric Corporation
Dates: 1972-1974

Weekend House
Location: Bear Creek, Pennsylvania
Client: Private
Dates: 1972-1974

F.M. Kirby Park
Location: Wilkes-Barre, Pennsylvania
Client: Wilkes-Barre Board of Recreation
Dates: 1973-1974

House
Location: Waverly, Pennsylvania
Client: Mr. and Mrs. Dorrance Belin
Dates: 1973-1975

Summer House
Location: West Cornwall, Connecticut
Client: Mr. and Mrs. Eric Q. Bohlin
Dates: 1973-1975

Ten East South Street Apartment Building
Location: Wilkes-Barre, Pennsylvania
Client: A.J. Grosek and Associates
Dates: 1973-1975

Downtown Urban Improvements
Public Square and South Main Street
Location: Wilkes-Barre, Pennsylvania
Client: City of Wilkes-Barre
Dates: 1973-1980

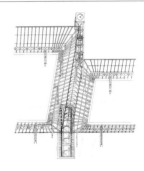

Coal Street Park Ice Rink
Location: Wilkes-Barre, Pennsylvania
Client: Wilkes-Barre Board of Recreation
Dates: 1974-1976

Charles Stewart Mott Gymnasium
Location: Troy, New York
Client: The Emma Willard School
Dates: 1974-1977

House Renovation

Location: Dallas, Pennsylvania
Client: Mr. and Mrs. Thomas Graham
Dates: 1977-1978

House

Location: Romansville, Pennsylvania
Client: Norman Gaffney
Dates: 1977-1980

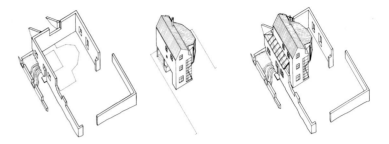

Conference Center

Location: Nanticoke, Pennsylvania
Client: Luzerne County Community College
Dates: 1978-1981

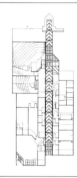

Program Center
Shelly Ridge Girl Scout Center

Location: Springfield Township, Pennsylvania
Client: Girl Scouts of Greater Philadelphia
Dates: 1979-1982

Swimming Pool and Bathhouse
Shelly Ridge Girl Scout Center

Location: Springfield Township, Pennsylvania
Client: Girl Scouts of Greater Philadelphia
Dates: 1979-1982

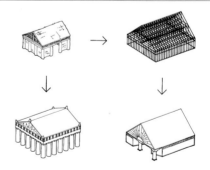

Caretaker's House
Shelly Ridge Girl Scout Center

Location: Springfield Township, Pennsylvania
Client: Girl Scouts of Greater Philadelphia
Dates: 1979-1983

House

Location: Jackson Township, Pennsylvania
Client: Mr. and Mrs. Charles Feldman
Dates: 1979-1984

Great Falls Historic District
Urban Improvements

Location: Paterson, New Jersey
Client: City of Paterson
Dates: 1980-1983

RPI Playhouse
Renovation and Expansion

Location: Troy, New York
Client: Rensselaer Polytechnic Institute
Dates: 1980-1983

Headquarters Building

Location: Wilkes-Barre, Pennsylvania
Client: InterMetro Industries Corporation
Dates: 1980-1984

Passenger Terminal
Harrisburg International Airport

Location: Middletown, Pennsylvania
Client: Commonwealth of Pennsylvania
Dates: 1981-1986

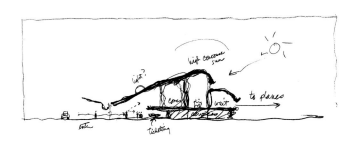

Elevator Testing Tower

Location: Randolph Township, New Jersey
Client: Westinghouse Electric Corporation
Dates: 1982-1984

H. Douglas Barclay Law Library
Location: Syracuse, New York
Client: Syracuse University
Dates: 1982-1984

House
Location: Annapolis, Maryland
Client: Mr. and Mrs. Alan Weitzman
Dates: 1982-1986

Ritter Park Playground and Rose Garden
Location: Huntington, West Virginia
Client: Greater Huntington Park and Recreation District
Dates: 1983-1986, 1992-1996

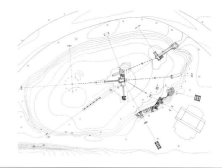

Master Plan and Design Manual
Philadelphia Zoological Garden
Location: Philadelphia, Pennsylvania
Client: Zoological Society of Philadelphia
Dates: 1983-1984

Freshmen Residence Halls and
Gateway Apartments
Location: Lewisburg, Pennsylvania
Client: Bucknell University
Dates: 1984-1986

House
Location: Bear Creek, Pennsylvania
Client: Bruce Barth and Joanna Douglas
Dates: 1984-1987

Software Engineering Institute
[Joint Venture with Burt Hill Kosar Rittelmann Associates]
Location: Pittsburgh, Pennsylvania
Client: Regional Industrial Development Corporation
of Southwestern Pennsylvania and Carnegie Mellon University
Dates: 1984-1987

Headquarters Building
Location: Indiana, Pennsylvania
Client: Royal Oil and Gas Corporation
Dates: 1985-1987

North Campus Townhouses and
Commons Building
Location: Ithaca, New York
Client: Cornell University
Dates: 1985-1987

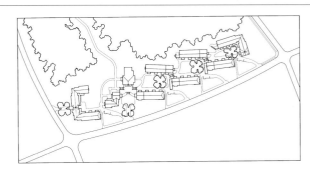

Expansion
The Judge Advocate General's School
Location: Charlottesville, Virginia
Client: University of Virginia
Dates: 1985-1990

Knott Athletic, Recreation
and Convocation Center
Location: Emmitsburg, Maryland
Client: Mount Saint Mary's College
Dates: 1986-1987

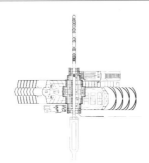

Melinda Cox District Library
and Headquarters
Location: Doylestown, Pennsylvania
Client: Bucks County
Dates: 1986-1988

Arthur Imperatore Library and Student Center
Location: Englewood, New Jersey
Client: Dwight-Englewood School
Dates: 1986-1988

Marts Athletic and Conference Center
Location: Wilkes-Barre, Pennsylvania
Client: Wilkes University
Dates: 1986-1988

Zig Zag Wren House
Location: Southampton, New York
Client: Parrish Art Museum
Date: 1987

Birdhouse Renovation
Philadelphia Zoological Garden
Location: Philadelphia, Pennsylvania
Client: Zoological Society of Philadelphia
Dates: 1987-1988

North School
Location: Hampton Township, Pennsylvania
Client: The Winchester Thurston School
Dates: 1987-1988, Phase I; 1989-1990, Phase II

Flood Residence Hall
Location: Wilkes-Barre, Pennsylvania
Client: King's College
Dates: 1987-1989

Lora and Alfred Flanagan Gymnasium
Location: Syracuse, New York
Client: Syracuse University
Dates: 1987-1989

Main Building Renovation and Expansion
Location: Salisbury, Connecticut
Client: Salisbury School
Dates: 1987-1989

Bogle Hall
Location: Blairstown, New Jersey
Client: Blair Academy
Dates: 1987-1990

Computer Research and Education Building
Location: Piscataway, New Jersey
Client: Rutgers University
Dates: 1987-1991

House in the Adirondacks
Location: New York State
Client: Private
Dates: 1987-1992

Carnivore Exhibits
Philadelphia Zoological Garden
Location: Philadelphia, Pennsylvania
Client: Zoological Society of Philadelphia
Dates: 1987-1995

Watson Residence Hall Expansion

Location: Syracuse, New York
Client: Syracuse University
Dates: 1988-1989

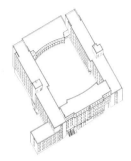

Center for Biotechnology and Bioengineering

Location: Pittsburgh, Pennsylvania
Client: University of Pittsburgh
Dates: 1988-1992

Sports and Entertainment Complex Study

Location: Mexico City, Mexico
Client: Private
Date: 1989

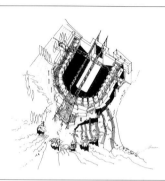

Day Residence Hall Expansion

Location: Syracuse, New York
Client: Syracuse University
Dates: 1989-1990

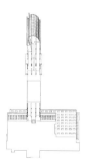

Eastern Sales and Operations Offices

Location: Pittsburgh, Pennsylvania
Client: NeXT Computer, Inc.
Dates: 1989-1990

Bensalem Municipal Building

Location: Bensalem Township, Pennsylvania
Client: Bensalem Township
Dates: 1989-1992

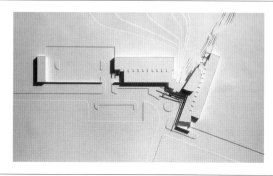

William G. McGowan School of Business

Location: Wilkes-Barre, Pennsylvania

Client: King's College

Dates: 1989-1992

Campus Master Plan

Location: Syracuse, New York

Client: Syracuse University

Date: 1990

Irving Avenue
Parking
Garage

Location: Syracuse,
New York

Client: Syracuse
University

Dates: 1990-1992

Residential Compound Garage

[Joint Venture with James Cutler Architects]

Location: Medina, Washington

Client: Private

Dates: 1990-1992

Residential Compound Guest House

[Joint Venture with James Cutler Architects]

Location: Medina, Washington

Client: Private

Dates: 1990-1993

Science and Mathematics Building

Location: St. Mary's City, Maryland

Client: St. Mary's College of Maryland

Dates: 1990-1993

Pennsylvania Higher Education Assistance Agency
Location: Harrisburg, Pennsylvania
Client: Capitol Commercial Corporation
Dates: 1990-1994

Residential Compound
[Joint Venture with James Cutler Architects]
Location: Medina, Washington
Client: Private
Dates: 1990-1995

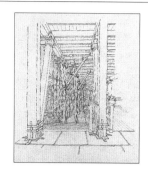

Samuel K. Faust Elementary School
Location: Bensalem, Pennsylvania
Client: Bensalem Township School District
Dates: 1991-1993

House
Location: Endless Mountains, Pennsylvania
Client: Buttonwood Farms
Dates: 1991-1994

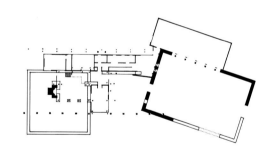

The Intelligent Workplace
Center for Building Performance
and Diagnostics
[Pierre Zoelly, Associated Architect]
Location: Pittsburgh, Pennsylvania
Client: Carnegie Mellon University &
Advanced Building Systems Integration Consortium
Dates: 1991-1994

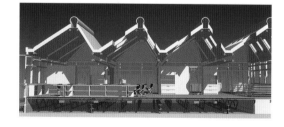

The Maxwell School, Eggers Hall
Location: Syracuse, New York
Client: Syracuse University
Dates: 1991-1994

Advanced Technology Classroom Building

Location: Media, Pennsylvania
Client: Delaware County Community College
Dates: 1991-1995

Speidel Gymnasium Expansion

Location: Elmira, New York
Client: Elmira College
Dates: 1991-1995

Headquarters and Scholars Center

Location: Research Triangle Park, North Carolina
Client: Sigma Xi, The Scientific Research Society
Dates: 1991-1996

North Campus Master Plan

Location: St. Mary's City, Maryland
Client: St. Mary's College of Maryland
Date: 1992

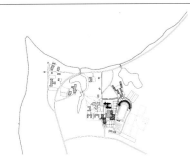

Pool Pavilion

Location: Montgomery County, Pennsylvania
Client: Private
Dates: 1992-1993

Carnegie Mellon Research Institute

Location: Pittsburgh, Pennsylvania
Client: Carnegie Mellon University
Dates: 1992-1994

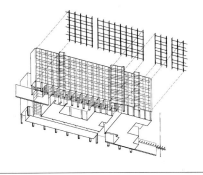

Clubhouse

Location: Huntsville, Pennsylvania
Client: Huntsville Golf Club
Dates: 1992-1994

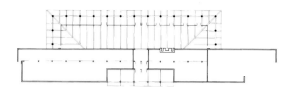

Lower School Library

Location: Forty Fort, Pennsylvania
Client: Wyoming Seminary
Dates: 1992-1994

Center for Educational Technologies

Location: Wheeling, West Virginia
Client: Wheeling Jesuit College
Dates: 1992-1994

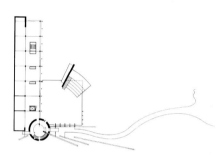

Weekend House

Location: Catoctin Mountains, Maryland
Client: Private
Dates: 1992-1994

Student Recreation Building

Location: Bloomsburg, Pennsylvania
Client: Bloomsburg University
Dates: 1992-1994

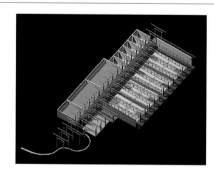

Townhouses

Location: St. Mary's City, Maryland
Client: St. Mary's College of Maryland
Dates: 1992-1994

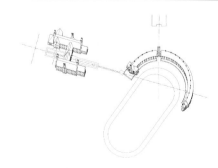

Pittsburgh Regional History Center
Location: Pittsburgh, Pennsylvania
Client: Western Pennsylvania Historical Society
Dates: 1992-1995

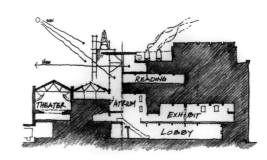

Children's Pavilion and
Fisher Gymnasium Restoration
Location: Silver Bay, New York
Client: Silver Bay Association
Dates: 1993-1994

Bede Lower School
Location: Englewood, New Jersey
Client: Dwight-Englewood School
Dates: 1993-1995

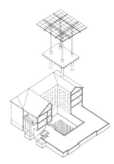

Sprague Hall Renovation
Location: Kingston, Pennsylvania
Client: Wyoming Seminary
Dates: 1993-1995

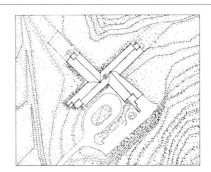

Mehoopany Elementary School
Location: Mehoopany Township, Pennsylvania
Client: Tunkhannock Area School District
Dates: 1993-1995

Classroom Building and Learning Center
Location: Philadelphia, Pennsylvania
Client: Temple University
Dates: 1993-1996

Firm History

Peter Q. Bohlin

Bernard J. Cywinski

Jon C. Jackson

Frank W. Grauman

W. Dan Haden, III

Firm History
Bohlin and Powell
1965-1977
Bohlin Powell Brown
1977-1979
Bohlin Powell Brown
Larkin Cywinski
1979-1980
Bohlin Powell
Larkin Cywinski
1980-1991
Bohlin Cywinski Jackson
1991

Offices
Wilkes-Barre, PA
Pittsburgh, PA
Philadelphia, PA
Seattle, WA

Principals
Peter Q. Bohlin
Bernard J. Cywinski
Jon C. Jackson
Frank W. Grauman
W. Dan Haden, III

Associates
Donald E. Maxwell
Russell B. Roberts
James A. Bell
Cornelius J. Reid, III
Michael F. Conner
Robert S. Pfaffmann
William D. Loose
C. Roxanne Sherbeck
Kenneth D. Mitchell
Allen H. Kachel

Staff
Edwin J. Gunshore, Jr.
Irene C. Martin
Kathleen M. Churnetski
Charles J. Cwenar
Natalie Gentile Wetmore
Annette J. Snyder
Karl A. Backus
Joseph P. Bridy
Marika S. Simms
Robin J. Kohles

Shari Ann Lersch
Stephen Altherr
Robert J. McLaughlin
Lee A. Clark
Jeffrey D. Wyant
Robert E. Miller
Terrence G. Wagner
Nancy Sokolove
Rebecca L. Boles
Joseph N. Biondo
Theresa W. Thomas
Gregory R. Mottola
Russell S. Hamlet
Sandra L. Coach
Michael D. Maiese
Christine M. Konnick
Adam Glaser
Alan K. Purvis
Monica M. Matushoneck
Erik W. Hokanson
Maria Keares Wyant
Stephanie Jacobs
Deborah R. Dechant
Shane Chandler
Peter C. Vonderlieth
Stephen A. George
Heather R. Woofter

Former Principals
Richard E. Powell
1965-1990
John F. Larkin
1979-1990
James D. Brown
1977-1980

Former Associates
William J. Gladish
Walter F. Blejwas
Ronald W. Huntsinger, Sr.

Former Staff
Christian Pegher
Paul R. Sirofchuck
Brian E. Polt
Kelly French Vresilovic
Richard A. Stokes
Keith H. Cochran
Joshua J. Cowder

Sharon M. Kasahara
Lawrence A. Newman
David J. Celento
Michael T. James
A. Todd Symonds
John Chong Hyeon Kim
Maria R. Segal
David G. Phillips
Michael J. Thomas
Terry J. Surjan
Grace K. Kuklinski
Gary Wong Wai-Choong
Stacie A. Sims
Barrett Feldman
Edward J. Kovaleski
Jeffrey T. Davis
Leonardo Diaz
Joann S. Gonchar
William A. Cook
David Ting Chee-Kiong
Lynn Coleman
Royce M. Earnest
James L. Dyson
Lynette M. Pollari
JoEllen C. Devers Bell
Bonnie Kemmerlin
Marian R. Olson
Jean M. Harrington
Lisa M. Hayes
Timothy Mock
Yun Hui Rorie Aaron
Eric Paul Reiwinkel
C. Joseph Cavanaugh
Rene D. Quinlan
Timothy S. Deal
Diane Carter
Adam F. Levy
Cathy Edgerly
Kevin Lew Shee-Chong
William D. Miller
Christopher D. Ross
Nancy J. Wintner
Georgina Lipsey
Dennis M. Cormier
Leo P. Karasinski
Robert S. Lewis
Margaret E. Bakker
Gerald N. Bucaccio
Carol A. Hasselmann
James S. Russell

Jon S. Norris
Joy Fay Landman
Lori Anne Montgomery
Jeffrey B. Averill
Hella Harasym
Elizabeth Stewart
Kathie J. Vezzani
Paula R. Maynes
Edward A. Barnhart
Patricia Devers
Roger G. Fortune
Michael D. Stoneking
Martin Anthony Rangel
Peter A. Matthews
Nancy G. Corwin
Stephen Von Storch
Christopher D. Macneal
Jennifer Pearson
Dennis M. Leach
John Patrick Barley
Andrew A. Blanda
Christopher Blood
Jeffery P. Gibbons
Katherine A. Costa
Kimberly A. Harris
Kathleen Hillis
Stephen Fritzinger
S. Scott Simmons
Taal Safdie
James Devers
Michael E. Peters
Paul S. DeCourt
Kyle Kinsman
Debra A. Hartman
Mark C. deShong
Joseph J. Salerno
Nestor Matthews
T. Jane Maloney
James C. Rogers
Steven E. Preiss
José Heraud
Joanne Chamberlin
Ronald E. Vanard
Lorie L. Mallik
Richard G. Williams
Scott T. Davis
Kenneth E. Redfoot
Joseph T. Cirillo
Gonzalo Rizzo-Patron
Duncan M. Penney

David H. Karp
John T. Coleman, Jr.
Robin J. Tufts
David G. Wilson
Serge Nalbantian
Joanne Schonfield
Yvonne M. Katerman
Gianne Conard
Barbara Friedman
Robert Marquardt
Robert E. Beckjord
Dana A. Riebling
Carl J. Handman
Debra T. Bayer
Joanne M. Hoffman
Eric J. Oliner
Jo Ellen Brewton
Harold Colker
Mary K. Donahoe
Robert A. Green
James R. Duffy
William A. Hope
William Hudak
Gilbert A. Rosenthal
Susan L. Nicholas
Philip Gray
Richard Shields
James Michaels
Ronald A. Wodaski
Herman L. Otto, Jr.
Candace Burnside
Harry C. Seargent
Eldra L. Anduze
David V. Lampman
Emil Jarolen
Margaret H. Price
Frank Burnside, Jr.
Lois A. Williams
Robert J. Klesius, Jr.
Judith L. Isely
Sarah M. Bragdon
James Cutler
Gregor D. Smith
William Wilcox
Klaus Chalupa
John Treiber
Karen Slean
Roy Wilson Lewis, Jr.
Christopher Speeth

Contributors

Joseph Esherick, the founding partner and a senior design principal at the San Francisco firm of Esherick Homsey Dodge and Davis received his Bachelor of Architecture degree from the University of Pennsylvania in 1937. His influence on Bay area architecture began to be felt in the early 1950s, when he joined the faculty of the University of California, Berkeley. Now Professor Emeritus of Architecture at Berkeley, he served as Chairman of the College of Environmental Design and later as Chairman of the Department of Architecture.

A Fellow of the American Institute of Architects, Joe Esherick has received the profession's most prestigious awards. In 1982, the Joint Award for Excellence in Architectural Education came from the AIA and the Association of Collegiate Schools of Architecture. In 1986, Esherick Homsey Dodge and Davis received the national Architecture Firm Award; in 1989, Mr. Esherick received the AIA's Gold Medal, and, in 1992, he was honored as the first Maybeck Award recipient by the California Council, American Institute of Architects.

Mack Scogin, Chairman of the Department of Architecture at Harvard University's Graduate School of Design and holder of the Kajima Chair, received a Bachelor of Architecture degree from Georgia Institute of Technology in 1967.

Before founding Scogin Elam and Bray Architects, Inc. in 1984, Mr. Scogin was associated with Heery and Heery Architects and Engineers, Inc. of Atlanta for over seventeen years. He was President and Chief Operating Officer, Director of Design when he resigned to form his own firm.

Based in Atlanta, Georgia, and noted internationally for their architecture, Scogin Elam and Bray have received American Institute of Architects National Honor Awards in 1988, 1989, 1992, and 1993. In 1989 they received the Silver Medal from the Atlanta Chapter of the American Institute of Architects in recognition of the firm's consistent pursuit and achievements in architectural design.

Photographers' Index